LECTIONARY WORSHIP AIDS

Series III, Cycle C

BY B. DAVID HOSTETTER

CSS Publishing Co., Inc.
Lima, Ohio

LECTIONARY WORSHIP AIDS, SERIES III, CYCLE C

Copyright © 1994 by
The CSS Publishing Company, Inc.
Lima, Ohio

You may copy the material in this publication if you are the original purchaser, for use as it was intended (worship material for worship use; educational material for classroom use; dramatic material for staging and production). No additional permission is required from the publisher for such copying by the original purchaser only. Inquiries should be addressed to: The CSS Publishing Company, Inc., 517 South Main Street, P.O. Box 4503, Lima, Ohio 45802-4503.

Library of Congress Cataloging-in-Publication Data
(Revised for volume 3)

Hostetter, B. David, 1926-
Lectionary worship aids. Series III.

Contents: Cycle A -- Cycle B -- Cycle C.
1. Worship programs. 2. Common lectionary (1992)
I. Title.
BV198.H66   1992   264'.34   92-29803
ISBN 1-55673-556-1 (v. 1)
ISBN 1-55673-622-3 (v. 2)
ISBN 0-7880-0076-4 (v. 3.)

Scripture quotations are from the *New Revised Standard Version of the Bible*, copyright 1989 by the Division of Christian Education of the National Council of the Churches of Christ in the USA. Used by permission.

This book is available in the following formats, listed by ISBN:
0-7880-0076-4   Book

PRINTED IN U.S.A.

Dedicated to the memory of my parents
The Reverend Benjamin Hess Hostetter and
Martha Elizabeth Taylor Hostetter,
both of whom taught me to pray
and used no prayer book except
the Holy Bible

TABLE OF CONTENTS

An Order of Worship 7

Advent
First Sunday In Advent 9
Second Sunday In Advent 11
Third Sunday In Advent 13
Fourth Sunday In Advent 15

Christmas
Christmas Eve/Day 17
Christmas Day (Additional Lections 2) 19
Christmas Day (Additional Lections 3) 21
First Sunday After Christmas 23
Second Sunday After Christmas 25
New Year's Eve/Day 28

Epiphany
Epiphany of the Lord 30
First Sunday After Epiphany 32
Second Sunday After Epiphany 34
Third Sunday After Epiphany 36
Fourth Sunday After Epiphany 38
Fifth Sunday After Epiphany 40
Sixth Sunday After Epiphany 42
Seventh Sunday After Epiphany 44
Eighth Sunday After Epiphany 46
Ninth Sunday After Epiphany 48
Last Sunday After Epiphany (Transfiguration) 50

Lent
Ash Wednesday 52
First Sunday In Lent 54
Second Sunday In Lent 56
Third Sunday In Lent 59
Fourth Sunday In Lent 61
Fifth Sunday In Lent 63
Sixth Sunday In Lent 65
Maundy Thursday 69

Easter
Easter Sunday	71
Second Sunday Of Easter	73
Third Sunday Of Easter	76
Fourth Sunday Of Easter	78
Fifth Sunday Of Easter	80
Sixth Sunday Of Easter	83
Ascension Day	85
Seventh Sunday Of Easter	87

Pentecost
Pentecost	89
Trinity Sunday	91
Proper 4	93
Proper 5	96
Proper 6	98
Proper 7	100
Proper 8	103
Proper 9	105
Proper 10	107
Proper 11	109
Proper 12	111
Proper 13	113
Proper 14	115
Proper 15	117
Proper 16	119
Proper 17	121
Proper 18	123
Proper 19	125
Proper 20	127
Proper 21	130
Proper 22	132
Proper 23	135
Proper 24	137
Proper 25	139
Proper 26	142
Proper 27	144
Proper 28	148
Christ The King	150
All Saints'	152
Thanksgiving	154
Index of the Scripture Passages	156
A note concerning lectionaries and calendars	160

AN ORDER OF WORSHIP

Prelude
*Call to Worship
Hymn of Praise, Psalm or Spiritual Song
*Prayer of Confession
*Declaration of Pardon and Exhortation
The Peace
First Lesson
*Psalm
Gloria Patri
Second Lesson
Gospel
*Prayer of the Day
Hymn
Sermon
Creed
*Prayer of Thanksgiving
Prayers of Intercession
Offering
*Prayer of Dedication
Hymn
The Benediction

* These parts of the service are spelled out for each Sunday of Year C in the pages of this book.

If you do not have this book in the pew, at least reproduce the Psalm for responsive or antiphonal reading. The Prayer of Confession and the Declaration of Pardon should also be reproduced for congregational reading and the Prayer of the Day. For maximum participation, the Prayer of Thanksgiving and the Prayer of Dedication may also be printed out.

FIRST SUNDAY IN ADVENT

Jeremiah 33:14-16   Psalm 25:1-10
1 Thessalonians 3:9-13   Luke 21:25-36

• CALL TO WORSHIP
Be vigilant, praying at all times for strength to pass safely through all imminent troubles and to stand in the presence of the Son of Man.

• PRAYER OF CONFESSION
God of all history, the passing of time sometimes escapes us. We live from payday to payday, from party to party, from crisis to crisis. We lose sight of our spiritual state of health until illness or tragedy brings us up short to take stock of ourselves again. We escape as we can from the social ills of our time, without seeing that they are signs of the times. Forgive our frequent indifference to the state of the nations and the immaturity of oursouls, for the sake of your perfect Son, Jesus of Nazareth. Amen.

• DECLARATION OF GOD'S FORGIVENESS
Hear the Good News! God is confirming your heartfelt belief so that you will stand faultless with all those who appear with Jesus before our Maker. Friends, believe the Good News! In Jesus Christ, we are forgiven.

• EXHORTATION
Keep awake and sober. The Son of Man is coming with great power and glory. Hold your heads high, for your liberation is near.

• PRAYER OF THE DAY
Eternal One, who was, who is, and who is to come, keep us aware of the meaning of events in our own lives and in our times. Save us from panic that hinders our doing anything constructive in society and thwarts personal growth. Be our ruler day by day. Amen.

• PRAYER OF THANKSGIVING
God of the prophets, righteous sovereign, Child of David's line, we rejoice in the branch of David that springs up and that buds and blossoms again and again with justice in Israel and in America. We are excited by every victory of truth over falsehood, every triumph of compassion over

indifference, every return to your war of those who have gone astray. We live in hope of the final perfection of your world in your time. Amen.

• PRAYER OF DEDICATION
God our Savior, we stand before you as those who are ready to be led by you in your way, to use what we have to clear the way for the coming of your goodness in full measure, through Mary's son, Jesus, and in the Spirit of the Christ. Amen.

• PSALM 25:1-10
To you, O LORD, I lift up my soul.
O my God, in you I trust; do not let me be put to shame;
do not let my enemies exult over me.
Do not let those who wait for you be put to shame;
let them be ashamed who are wantonly treacherous.
Make me to know your ways, O LORD; teach me your paths.
Lead me in your truth, and teach me,
for you are the God of my salvation;
for you I wait all day long.
Be mindful of your mercy, O LORD,
and of your steadfast love,
for they have been from of old.
Do not remember the sins of my youth or my transgressions;
according to your steadfast love remember me,
for your goodness' sake, O LORD!
Good and upright is the LORD;
therefore he instructs sinners in the way.
He leads the humble in what is right,
and teaches the humble his way.
All the paths of the LORD are steadfast love and faithfulness,
for those who keep his covenant and his decrees.

SECOND SUNDAY IN ADVENT

Malachi 3:1-4 or Baruch 5:1-9　　　　　　　　　Luke 1:68-79
Philippians 1:3-11　　　　　　　　　　　　　　Luke 3:1-6

• CALL TO WORSHIP
Get the road ready for the royal visit: make a straight path for Christ to travel! The winding roads must be made straight and the rough places smooth. All humanity shall see God's salvation.

• PRAYER OF CONFESSION
Holy God, Messenger of the new covenant, flaming Spirit, we confess that we are sinners and cannot worship you worthily except as we are purified and cleansed of our sins. Let your Holy Fire refine our characters not merely our appearance, so that our very natures can become true and rich, purged of the dross of our deepest faults and the evil that corrupts us. Fit both pastor and people to worship you in the purity appropriate to the house of God, through the fire of the Holy Spirit. Amen.

• DECLARATION OF GOD'S FORGIVENESS
Hear the Good News! The One who started the good work in you will bring it to completion by the Day of Christ Jesus. Friends, believe the Good News. In Jesus Christ, we are forgiven.

• EXHORTATION
Grow richer in love, in knowledge and insight of every kind, then on the Day of Christ, you will be flawless and without blame, reaping the full harvest of goodness that comes through Jesus Christ to the glory of God.

• PRAYER OF THE DAY
In this year of our Lord, in this day of our times, Speaker-Out-of-Eternity, let your word be heard again, that every baptism may be a sign of repentance for the forgiveness of sins, and the wilderness of modern life bloom with the flowers of goodness and peace. Amen.

• PRAYER OF THANKSGIVING
Turner-of-tides, you have done great things for us and we are glad indeed. Out of illness we have found new health. Out of sorrow we have found new rivers of joy. In barren places we have planted seeds that you

bring to a harvest of goodness. Out of spiritual poverty you have restored our fortune and made us rich in Christ. All praise to you! We sing for you! Amen.

• **PRAYER OF DEDICATION**
Receive, Divine Harvester, our offerings as seed-money that enables the sowing of the seed of the word in this place and to the ends of the earth. Use us as your hired hands, busy both in sowing and in harvesting, for the sake of Christ's church. Amen.

• **Psalm: Luke 1:68-79 The Benedictus**
"Blessed be the Lord God of Israel,
for he has looked favorably on his people and redeemed them.
He has raised up a mighty savior for us in the house of his servant David,
as he spoke through the mouth of his holy prophets from of old,
that we would be saved from our enemies
and from the hand of all who hate us.
Thus he has shown the mercy promised to our ancestors,
and has remembered his holy covenant,
the oath that he swore to our ancestor Abraham,
to grant us that we, being rescued from the hands of our
enemies, might serve him without fear,
in holiness and righteousness before him all our days.
And you, child, will be called the prophet of the Most High;
for you will go before the Lord to prepare his ways,
to give knowledge of salvation to his people
by the forgiveness of their sins.
By the tender mercy of our God,
the dawn from on high will break upon us,
to give light to those who sit in darkness and in the shadow
of death, to guide our feet into the way of peace."

THIRD SUNDAY IN ADVENT

Zephaniah 3:14-20   Isaiah 12:2-6
Philippians 4:4-7   Luke 3:7-18

• CALL TO WORSHIP
Express gratitude to God, invoking God by name. Make God's deeds known in the world around, declaring the supremacy of the divine name.

• PRAYER OF CONFESSION
God of peace, Prince of peace, Spirit of peace, your names are to be hallowed as supreme. Forgive us if we fail to give due honor to your name in our families and in our social life. In our society the name of Santa Claus sometimes obscures the name of the Christ Child, the hammering of elves drowns out the song of angels. The mission of reindeer competes with the adoration of shepherds and the travel of those who seek the one born to be king. Pardon us if we have let such things get out of hand in our social circles. Help us to restore your name to its rightful place. Amen.

• DECLARATION OF GOD'S FORGIVENESS
Hear the Good News! The peace of God, which is beyond our utmost understanding, will keep guard over your hearts and your thoughts, in Christ Jesus. Friends, believe the Good News! In Jesus Christ, we are forgiven.

• EXHORTATION
Now my friends, all that is true, all that is noble, all that is just and pure, all that is lovable and gracious, whatever is excellent and admirable—fill all your thoughts with these things.

• PRAYER OF THE DAY
God of wisdom, God-in-action, Spirit of inquiry, prompt us to ask not only what we should believe but what should we do? Save us from fruitless speculation that does not issue in obedient action to fulfill our vocation to serve you in the serving of others. Amen.

• PRAYER OF THANKSGIVING
Magnanimous God, to the cries for help we have made in anxious moments, and the petitions we have offered in times of need, we add our

thanksgivings and our expressions of joy. We have joy in the Lord because you have enabled us to put into practice some of the lessons that Jesus and the apostles have taught us, and to follow the good example of others, old and young, who have also been following Christ. We have no higher joy than the sense of your presence and the love you show us again and again. Amen.

• PRAYER OF DEDICATION
Holy One of Israel, Christ of the church, we gather here as sons and daughters of the faithful, to make our deeds known in the community where we live, and to declare that your name is supreme. We depart to take our cup of joy to share with others, in the name of Jesus. Amen.

• PSALM - Isaiah 12:2-6
Surely God is my salvation;
I will trust, and will not be afraid,
for the LORD GOD is my strength and my might;
he has become my salvation.
With joy you will draw water from the wells of salvation.
And you will say in that day: Give thanks to the LORD,
call on his name; make known his deeds among the nations;
proclaim that his name is exalted.
Sing praises to the LORD, for he has done gloriously;
let this be known in all the earth.
Shout aloud and sing for joy, O royal Zion,
for great in your midst is the Holy One of Israel.

FOURTH SUNDAY IN ADVENT

Micah 5:2-5a Luke 1:47-55 or Psalm 80:1-7
Hebrews 10:5-10 Luke 1:39-55

• CALL TO WORSHIP
After the example of Jesus Christ in his coming, present yourselves before God, saying: "I have come to do your will, O God."

• PRAYER OF CONFESSION
God of surprises, you bring your name of peace out of a small clan and a previously insignificant place. Forgive us if we look for leaders for our era only in places of wealth and cities of power. If we have stood in the way of those you have called to be shepherds of your flock because they did not seem imposing and appeared in humility we are sorry. We need to learn to measure greatness as you do, as manifest in Jesus Christ, in whose name we pray. Amen.

• DECLARATION OF GOD'S FORGIVENESS
Hear the Gracious News! God has not resisted the prayers of the people. He has made his face shine on us in Jesus Christ, that we may be saved. Friends, believe the Good News! In Jesus Christ, we are forgiven.

• EXHORTATION
Recount what you have been told about this child Jesus, and share the real meaning of what has happened in Bethlehem.

• PRAYER OF THE DAY
Give us joy in believing, God our Savior, that as you have kept past promises, you will also fulfill those for the future made by your Son, Jesus Christ. Give us joy in believing that our children and grandchildren may live to see that great day if it does not come in ours. Amen.

• PRAYER OF THANKSGIVING
Responsive God, you have restored your people who have called upon you. We have prayed that you would make your face shine upon us, that we might be saved. Your response has been to become human for humanity's salvation. We rejoice with the apostle that we have seen the light of the knowledge of the glory of God in the face of Jesus Christ. With

Elizabeth we share the wonder, "Who are we, that the mother of our Lord should be one of us?" With blessed Mary, we rejoice in God our Savior. Amen.

• **PRAYER OF DEDICATION**
Receive your church standing before you, O God, as a body prepared to be moved by the Spirit to do your will in our time and in this place. Amen.

• **PSALM: LUKE 1:47-55**
My spirit rejoices in God my Savior,
for he has looked with favor on the lowliness of his servant.
Surely, from now on all generations will call me blessed;
for the Mighty One has done great things for me, and holy is his name.
His mercy is for those who fear him
from generation to generation.
He has shown strength with his arm;
he has scattered the proud in the thoughts of their hearts.
He has brought down the powerful from their thrones,
and lifted up the lowly;
he has filled the hungry with good things, and sent the rich away empty.
He has helped his servant Israel, in remembrance of his mercy,
according to the promise he made to our ancestors, to Abraham and to his descendants forever.

(or)
• **PSALM 80:1-7**
Give ear, O Shepherd of Israel,
you who lead Joseph like a flock!
You who are enthroned upon the cherubim,
shine forth before Ephraim and Benjamin and Manasseh.
Stir up your might,
and come to save us!
Restore us, O God;
let your face shine, that we may be saved.
O LORD God of hosts,
how long will you be angry with your people's prayers?
You have fed them with the bread of tears,
and given them tears to drink in full measure.
You make us the scorn of our neighbors;
our enemies laugh among themselves.
Restore us, O God of hosts;
let your face shine, that we may be saved.

CHRISTMAS EVE/DAY

Isaiah 9:2-7   Psalm 96
Titus 2:11-14   Luke 2:1-14 (15-20)

• CALL TO WORSHIP
Silence, everyone, in the presence of God, who has come out of the sanctuary of heaven.

• PRAYER OF CONFESSION
God of all worlds, ours seems at times like an abandoned one. We share in its sin, its darkness and its despair. We feel that you have left us alone to find our own way out of the mess we have made of things. We have forgotten that the world was created by you, re-visited by you in Jesus Christ, and is still yours, a dwelling place of your choice for your Spirit. Forgive the belief that you are nowhere, that forgets that you are now here, in the Spirit of Jesus Christ. Amen.

• DECLARATION OF GOD'S FORGIVENESS
Hear the Good News! The Lord has come, and is coming again. Let the peace of God keep guard over your hearts and your thoughts, in Christ Jesus. Friends, believe the Good News! In Jesus Christ, we are forgiven.

• EXHORTATION
The Lord is near. Have no anxiety, but in everything make your requests known to God in prayer and petition with thanksgiving.

• PRAYER OF THE DAY
Child of Bethlehem, Man of Nazareth, Christ of God, with Mary we treasure the stories of your birth and ponder over these things. May the celebration of your birth, both in this place and in our social circles, bring glory and praise to your name. Amen.

• PRAYER OF THANKSGIVING
Shepherd of Israel, Lamb of God, Keeper of Christ's flock, with Bethlehem shepherds of old, we come to see what has happened and consider what has been made known to us. We rejoice in the birth of this child Jesus who embodies both the good Shepherd and the Lamb of God that takes away the sin of the world. For his obedience to your saving purpose we are thankful. That you

become involved in the sin and suffering of our world, we are astonished. That you continue to draw us together as your flock by the Spirit we are comforted. Amen.

• PRAYER OF DEDICATION
Not often enough, O God, do we offer you the gift of our silence, in adoration, in attentiveness, in anticipation of your directions. Receive us in this solemn moment, and in such times of silence as we find for you in the days to come. Amen.

• PSALM 96
O sing to the LORD a new song;
sing to the LORD, all the earth.
Sing to the LORD, bless his name;
tell of his salvation from day to day.
Declare his glory among the nations,
his marvelous works among all the peoples.
For great is the LORD, and greatly to be praised;
he is to be revered above all gods.
For all the gods of the peoples are idols,
but the LORD made the heavens.
Honor and majesty are before him;
strength and beauty are in his sanctuary.
Ascribe to the LORD, O families of the peoples,
ascribe to the LORD glory and strength.
Ascribe to the LORD the glory due his name;
bring an offering, and come into his courts.
Worship the LORD in holy splendor;
tremble before him, all the earth.
Say among the nations, "The LORD is king!
The world is firmly established;
it shall never be moved.
He will judge the peoples with equity."
Let the heavens be glad,
and let the earth rejoice;
let the sea roar, and all that fills it;
let the field exult, and everything in it.
Then shall all the trees of the forest sing for joy before the LORD;
for he is coming, for he is coming to judge the earth.
He will judge the world with righteousness,
and the peoples with his truth.

CHRISTMAS DAY 2

Isaiah 62:6-12   Psalm 97
Titus 3:4-7   Luke 2:(1-7) 8-20

• CALL TO WORSHIP
I have Good News for you: there is great joy coming to the whole people. Today in the city of David a deliverer has been born to you - the Messiah, the Christ.

• PRAYER OF CONFESSION
God of the gospel, whose glory brightens the night sky on Christmas eve, and the birth of whose Son in Bethlehem brings the dawn of a new day, hear our prayers for forgiveness and mercy. Pardon us if we have made idols of what are only symbols of the coming of Jesus, if traditional practice rather than the reality of the coming of Jesus Christ, has defined the meaning of today. We can appeal to your kindness and generosity, not because of any good deeds of our own, but because of our salvation through the water of baptism and the renewing power of the Holy Spirit. By your grace, Jesus Christ is our Savior. Amen.

• DECLARATION OF GOD'S FORGIVENESS
Hear the Good News! God in highest heaven grants peace on earth to all on whom rests the favor of the Most High. Friends, believe the Good News! In Jesus Christ we are forgiven.

• EXHORTATION
Raise a signal to all people. This is God's proclamation to earth's farthest bounds.

• PRAYER OF THE DAY
Exalted One, having received the good news of Jesus Christ with great joy, we would be sent like the shepherds to astonish others with the story of Jesus and the meaning of our salvation through his grace. Amen.

• PRAYER OF THANKSGIVING
God in highest heaven, we give you thanks for the sending of Jesus Christ into our world to be a gift of peace, a person of peace, a prince of peace. Christ most lowly, we give thanks for your humble birth and gracious life, for salvation and the hope of eternal life. Spirit most holy, we thank you

for the water of rebirth and the renewal of the Spirit thus signified, by which we are saved, being justified by the grace of our Lord Jesus Christ. All glory be ascribed to you, God, Giving, Coming, Renewing. Amen.

• PRAYER OF DEDICATION
Holy Child of God and of Mary Virgin, heaven and earth are your homes, temple and stable are hallowed by your presence. We bring our gifts to you so that the good news of peace may continue to sound in earth and heaven, echoed by human voices, the voice of your church. Amen.

• PSALM 97:1-12
The LORD is king! Let the earth rejoice;
let the many coastlands be glad!
Clouds and thick darkness are all around him;
righteousness and justice are the foundation of his throne.
Fire goes before him,
and consumes his adversaries on every side.
His lightnings light up the world;
the earth sees and trembles.
The mountains melt like wax before the LORD,
before the Lord of all the earth.
The heavens proclaim his righteousness;
and all the peoples behold his glory.
All worshipers of images are put to shame,
those who make their boast in worthless idols;
all gods bow down before him.
Zion hears and is glad,
and the towns of Judah rejoice,
because of your judgments, O God.
For you, O LORD, are most high over all the earth;
you are exalted far above all gods.
The LORD loves those who hate evil;
he guards the lives of his faithful;
he rescues them from the hand of the wicked.
Light dawns for the righteous,
and joy for the upright in heart.
Rejoice in the LORD, O you righteous,
and give thanks to his holy name!

CHRISTMAS DAY 3

Isaiah 52:7-10   Psalm 98
Hebrews 1:1-4 (5-12)   John 1:1-14

• CALL TO WORSHIP
Receive Jesus Christ, who is the WORD made flesh, and who has come to dwell among us, full of grace and truth.

• PRAYER OF CONFESSION
True God, Gracious God, we are still enticed to idolatry. We are fascinated by glamorous stars. We are taken in by false propaganda. We are frightened by the threats of the politically and economically powerful. We lose confidence in your pledge to preserve the lives of your saints. We forget that you love those who hate evil and resist it. Forgive our misplaced confidence, our faith in the wrong powers. Restore our joy in the gentle qualities of truth and grace made personal in Jesus Christ. Amen.

• DECLARATION OF GOD'S FORGIVENESS
Hear the Good News! In Christ our release is secured and our sins are forgiven through the shedding of his blood. In receiving God's only Son, you have been received as a child of God. Friends, believe the Good News! In Jesus Christ, we are forgiven.

• EXHORTATION
Bear witness to the light of grace and truth that you have seen in Jesus Christ. There are others who have not yet recognized him as the real light that enlightens everyone coming into the world.

• PRAYER OF THE DAY
Mender of our broken world, enable us as members of your family to be cooperative agents in the restoration of the unity of all things in Christ, all things in heaven and earth. Then will all the earth be glad and the stars sing for joy. Amen.

• PRAYER OF THANKSGIVING
We hail your coming, invisible Sovereign, incarnate Prince, powerful Spirit. We rejoice with apostles who lived in the historic days of Jesus Christ, your Son, and with prophets who anticipated that day. With all

your earthly realm we join our voices in praise of the glory revealed in Jesus Christ. We run with the good news of the reunification of all things around your beloved. We praise you for all the spiritual blessings that you give us, here and hereafter. Amen.

• **PRAYER OF DEDICATION**
We renew our allegiance to you, God's Child, acknowledging our adoption as your brothers and sisters. We pledge our resources and ourselves, that the light shall shine on and the darkness never overwhelm it. Amen.

• **PSALM 98**
O sing to the LORD a new song,
for he has done marvelous things.
His right hand and his holy arm have gotten him victory.
The LORD has made known his victory;
he has revealed his vindication in the sight of the nations.
He has remembered his steadfast love and faithfulness
to the house of Israel.
All the ends of the earth have seen the victory of our God.
Make a joyful noise to the LORD, all the earth;
break forth into joyous song and sing praises.
Sing praises to the LORD with the lyre,
with the lyre and the sound of melody.
With trumpets and the sound of the horn
make a joyful noise before the King, the LORD.
Let the sea roar, and all that fills it;
the world and those who live in it.
Let the floods clap their hands;
let the hills sing together for joy
at the presence of the LORD,
for he is coming to judge the earth.
He will judge the world with righteousness,
and the peoples with equity.

FIRST SUNDAY AFTER CHRISTMAS

1 Samuel 2:18-20, 26　　　　　　　　　　　　　Psalm 148
Colossians 3:12-17　　　　　　　　　　　　　　Luke 2:41-52

• **CALL TO WORSHIP**
Give thanks to our Sovereign with your whole heart, in the assembly of the upright, in the company of the entire congregation.

• **PRAYER OF CONFESSION**
Ageless God, forgive us if we have kept the young from worshiping with us by our insistence on old ways of worship and our refusal to accept new words and new music that can involve children and youth with us in our gathering. Excuse our demands for stillness and silence that ignore your acceptance of children in their simplicity and sincerity. By the examples of Samuel and Jesus, open our minds to the service that can be rendered to you by the young in years and the young in heart. Amen.

• **DECLARATION OF GOD'S FORGIVENESS**
Hear the Good News! God has forgiven you so let the peace of Christ abide in your heart. Friends, believe the Good News! In Jesus Christ, we are forgiven.

• **EXHORTATION**
As you have been forgiven, be forgiving, compassionate, kind, humble, gentle, patient, preserving the unity of the church as the body of Christ.

• **PRAYER OF THE DAY**
Child of God and child with human parents, teach us to grow in wisdom, both by listening and by asking questions. Help us to keep in proper balance our duties to the church family and our own households that we too may increase in favor with God and our peers. Amen.

• **PRAYER OF THANKSGIVING**
Mind beyond our knowing, we praise you for revealing what we should know in Jesus Christ. Treasure beyond our possessing, we give thanks, that for the sake of our enrichment, Christ shared human poverty to put divine wealth within our reach. Maker of history, who can trace your

purposes? We marvel at your ways with humanity, and live in suspense as to the future you point to in Jesus Christ, Child of history, Child of eternity. Amen.

• **PRAYER OF DEDICATION**
We are not so foolish, wise God, as to believe that we can buy your favor with these gifts. We make our offering and present ourselves a living sacrifice, that your will be done on earth as in heaven. Amen.

• **PSALM 148**
Praise the LORD! Praise the LORD from the heavens;
praise him in the heights!
Praise him, all his angels;
praise him, all his host!
Praise him, sun and moon;
praise him, all you shining stars!
Praise him, you highest heavens,
and you waters above the heavens!
Let them praise the name of the LORD,
for he commanded and they were created.
He established them forever and ever;
he fixed their bounds, which cannot be passed.
Praise the LORD from the earth, you sea monsters and all deeps,
fire and hail, snow and frost, stormy wind fulfilling his command!
Mountains and all hills,
fruit trees and all cedars!
Wild animals and all cattle,
creeping things and flying birds!
Kings of the earth and all peoples,
princes and all rulers of the earth!
Young men and women alike,
old and young together!
Let them praise the name of the LORD,
for his name alone is exalted;
his glory is above earth and heaven.
He has raised up a horn for his people,
praise for all his faithful,
for the people of Israel who are close to him.
Praise the LORD!

SECOND SUNDAY AFTER CHRISTMAS

Jeremiah 31:7-14　　　　　　　　　　　Psalm 147:12-20
or Sirach 24:1-12　　　　　　　or Wisdom of Solomon 10:15-21
Ephesians 1:3-14　　　　　　　　　　　　John 1:(1-9) 10-18

• **CALL TO WORSHIP**
Sing out your praises and say,
God has saved his people.
See how the Savior brings them from the end of the earth,
The blind and lame among them,
Women with child
And women in labor, a great company.
Young men and old shall rejoice,
Then shall the girl show her joy in the dance.
God turns their mourning into gladness,
And gives them joy to outdo their sorrow.

• **PRAYER OF CONFESSION**
All-glorious God, paternal, fraternal, maternal, though we have faith in Jesus Christ, and love towards your people yet we are not without blemish in your sight, not full of love, wisdom, and other spiritual blessings you still have available for us. Our love is not as inclusive as yours, and there is much we need to learn. Give us clearer vision of all that we are meant to be, so that by becoming fulfilled, we may increase the glory that is properly revealed in Jesus Christ, your beloved. Amen.

• **DECLARATION OF GOD'S FORGIVENESS**
Hear the Good News! The liberator has come to free us from all proud pretenses. The Christ has come in Jesus of Nazareth to show us the undeserved favor of God. Friends, believe the Good News! In Jesus Christ we are forgiven.

• **EXHORTATION**
Accept the limitations of your own knowledge. Have reverence for the wisdom of the Creator. Be thankful for his love in Christ and for a humble place in his house.

• **PRAYER OF THE DAY**
Available God, whatever our age, whether married or single, make us sensitive to what you are doing and about to do, that we may not miss the

excitement of being a part of the living history that you are writing, through Jesus Christ. Amen.

• **PRAYER OF THANKSGIVING**
We give thanks, God of Job and Jeremiah, David's Lord, Anna's Christ, Luke's savior, that we have found your house in many places. We have found places of prayer with the swallows and the sparrows. We have sung your praise in a quiet circle under the stars. We have enjoyed the choir of many voices and the joyous sounds of musical instruments and found inspiration and refreshment. Along our pilgrim way you provide the cup that sustains both soul and body. We are happy when we trust in you. Amen.

• **PRAYER OF DEDICATION**
God of all places, many of us return to this place again and again, expecting spiritual refreshment and growth in grace. Bless all that we do to make this a place of renewal for all who will come to Jesus Christ. Amen.

• **PSALM 147:12-20**
Praise the LORD, O Jerusalem!
Praise your God, O Zion!
For he strengthens the bars of your gates;
he blesses your children within you.
He grants peace within your borders;
he fills you with the finest of wheat.
He sends out his command to the earth;
his word runs swiftly.
He gives snow like wool;
he scatters frost like ashes.
He hurls down hail like crumbs
—who can stand before his cold?
He sends out his word, and melts them;
he makes his wind blow, and the waters flow.
He declares his word to Jacob,
his statutes and ordinances to Israel.
He has not dealt thus with any other nation;
they do not know his ordinances.
Praise the LORD!

(or)

• WISDOM 10:15-21
A holy people and blameless race
wisdom delivered from a nation of oppressors.
She entered the soul of a servant of the Lord,
and withstood dread kings with wonders and signs.
She gave to holy people the reward of their labors;
she guided them along a marvelous way,
and became a shelter to them by day,
and a starry flame through the night.
She brought them over the Red Sea,
and led them through deep waters;
but she drowned their enemies,
and cast them up from the depth of the sea.
Therefore the righteous plundered the ungodly;
they sang hymns, O Lord, to your holy name,
and praised with one accord your defending hand;
for wisdom opened the mouths of those who were mute,
and made the tongues of infants speak clearly.

NEW YEAR'S EVE/DAY

Ecclesiastes 3:1-13   Psalm 8
Revelation 21:1-6a   Matthew 25:31-46

- **CALL TO WORSHIP**

Worship God, our Sovereign, with reverence for the majesty of God's name in all the earth!

- **PRAYER OF CONFESSION**

God before time, God in our time, God Eternal, you mark our days and years for what we have experienced and what we have learned. You give us time to develop characters shaped by joy and sorrow. We do not always learn willingly and change our ways to follow the way of Jesus Christ. Pardon our stubbornness and give us further time to learn and improve our times for the sake of your perfect Son, Jesus Christ. Amen.

- **DECLARATION OF GOD'S FORGIVENESS**

Hear the Good News! We have been given time to reconsider our ways and to prepare ourselves for the day of judgment yet to come. Friends, believe the Good News! In Jesus Christ, we are forgiven.

- **EXHORTATION**

Feed the hungry; give drink to the thirsty; welcome strangers; clothe the naked; visit the sick and prisoners; you will be ready for the day of reckoning.

- **PRAYER OF THE DAY**

Open our eyes, Divine Healer, that we may see your face in the faces of the poor, the sick and the prisoner and in caring for them give homage to you, our Savior and Friend. Amen.

- **PRAYER OF THANKSGIVING**

Unchanging God, Contemporary Christ, ageless Spirit, for all that you teach us in the course of life we give thanks. We are grateful for what you provide for us to eat and drink and for the pleasures of meaningful work. We enjoy times of recreation and love making. We anticipate the end of hate and war and want. We look for the defaced to be removed with the coming of the new heaven and earth in which there is love perfected, peace with justice and plenty shared generously. Hasten the time of healing when we can live together without fear or misunderstanding in your new heaven and earth under the banner of love. Glory to God, *drying tears, ending suffering, sharing glory. Amen.*

• PRAYER OF DEDICATION
God of the past year, God of today, God of this new year, receive the offerings that we bring and the service we pledge not only for your worship in this place but for ministry to those in need; for Christ's sake. Amen.

• PSALM 8
O LORD, our Sovereign, how majestic is your name in all the earth!
You have set your glory above the heavens.
Out of the mouths of babes and infants you have founded a bulwark because of your foes,
to silence the enemy and the avenger.
When I look at your heavens, the work of your fingers,
the moon and the stars that you have established;
what are human beings that you are mindful of them,
mortals that you care for them?
Yet you have made them a little lower than God,
and crowned them with glory and honor.
You have given them dominion over the works of your hands;
you have put all things under their feet,
all sheep and oxen, and also the beasts of the field,
the birds of the air, and the fish of the sea,
whatever passes along the paths of the seas.
O LORD, our Sovereign, how majestic is your name in all the earth!

EPIPHANY OF THE LORD

Isaiah 60:1-6   Psalm 72:1-7, 10-14
Ephesians 3:1-12   Matthew 2:1-12

• **CALL TO WORSHIP**
Give homage to the Christ. Bring him your treasures and offer him your gifts.

• **PRAYER OF CONFESSION**
God of justice and peace, for some of us it is difficult to determine whether we are among the oppressors or the oppressed. We declare our belief in justice, but are concerned mostly for our own rights and not always for the rights of others. Your anointed One comes to help those who are needy and to give judgment for the suffering. Though we are loyal to him in principle we are not always with him in practice. Forgive such hypocrisy, for Jesus' sake. Amen.

• **DECLARATION OF GOD'S FORGIVENESS**
Hear the Good News! Through Jesus Christ, we who are not Jews may also share with them God's promise. Friends, believe the Good News! In Jesus Christ, we are forgiven.

• **EXHORTATION**
Pass on the Good News. It is no longer a secret to be kept from anyone. The whole human race may be part of the body of Christ, His Church.

• **PRAYER OF THE DAY**
Give us the courage, Divine Ruler, if ever we must choose between obedience to earthly or heavenly monarch, to be obedient to the heavenly vision. Free us from being yoked with any oppressor, that we may be among the nations that march toward your light, shining in Jesus Christ. Amen.

• **PRAYER OF THANKSGIVING**
We rejoice with the prophet, your prophet, O God, who sees the vision of the new Jerusalem. We look for the day when the city of God on earth will be the gathering of the world's children in a city of light. Though there is darkness covering the earth and dark night the nations, the glory, your glory, shall appear. To your presence will march the nations, and

rulers to your rising with the radiance of the sun. *In such visions that lighten our darkness, we are overjoyed like the Magi in seeing the star.* Amen.

• **PRAYER OF DEDICATION**
Gold, frankincense and myrrh are not our gifts but what we have is yours to use, O Christ, in the support of your church and in the service of others. Amen.

• **PSALM 72:1-7,10-14**
Give the king your justice, O God,
and your righteousness to a king's son.
May he judge your people with righteousness,
and your poor with justice.
May the mountains yield prosperity for the people,
and the hills, in righteousness.
May he defend the cause of the poor of the people,
give deliverance to the needy, and crush the oppressor.
May he live while the sun endures,
and as long as the moon, throughout all generations.
May he be like rain that falls on the mown grass,
like showers that water the earth.
In his days may righteousness flourish and peace abound,
until the moon is no more.
May the kings of Tarshish and of the isles render him tribute,
may the kings of Sheba and Seba bring gifts.
May all kings fall down before him,
all nations give him service.
For he delivers the needy when they call,
the poor and those who have no helper.
He has pity on the weak and the needy,
and saves the lives of the needy.
From oppression and violence he redeems their life;
and precious is their blood in his sight.

FIRST SUNDAY AFTER THE EPIPHANY

Isaiah 43:1-7   Psalm 29
Acts 8:14-17   Luke 3:15-17, 21-22

• **CALL TO WORSHIP**
Praise God's glorious name, bow down before the Holy One when Christ appears.

• **PRAYER OF CONFESSION**
Magnificent Creator, we are humbled by the voice of your power and majesty. Even your Son Jesus awes us, as he does your servant, John the Baptist, so that we know we are unworthy to unfasten his shoes. We are often too proud to stoop to the menial service that our neighbor's needs require. Forgive the arrogance that overlooks the Christ when he is in the guise of our needy neighbors anywhere in the world; through Jesus Christ, your model son. Amen.

• **DECLARATION OF GOD'S FORGIVENESS**
Friends, hear the Good News. We share the promise of God with his people the Jews, through the secret of Christ. Though we are unworthy, we are granted God's favor also in Jesus Christ, and are baptized into the church of His beloved Son. Friends, believe the Good News. In Jesus Christ, we are forgiven.

• **ADMONITION**
Do not lose heart. Proclaim the Good New of the riches of Christ to all, so that the wisdom of God in all its varied forms may be known by everyone.

• **PRAYER OF THE DAY**
Creator Divine, you have planted the seed of the word within us, so that we may be wheat for your granary. Drench us with the good rain of your Spirit so that we may be part of your abundant harvest to be gathered into your heavenly granary, and not chaff to be destroyed as worthless; through the grace of your worthy Son, Jesus of Nazareth. Amen.

• **PRAYER OF THANKSGIVING**
Gracious God, you send your Anointed to bring good news to the poor, to heal the broken-hearted, to announce release to the captives and

freedom to those in prison. Such salvation turns sadness into joy and mourning into gladness. So we sing your praise and give thanks to you from sincere hearts, for even in the midst of earth's ruins you help us to rebuild with hope. Amen.

• PRAYER OF DEDICATION
You are our monarch forever, O God. We worship you in the presentation of our offerings. Mighty God, give strength to your people, that they may serve you always. Gracious God, bless your people with peace, that they may be peacemakers in a world of strife; through Jesus, Prince of peace. Amen.

• PSALM 29
Ascribe to the LORD, O heavenly beings,
ascribe to the LORD glory and strength.
Ascribe to the LORD the glory of his name;
worship the LORD in holy splendor.
The voice of the LORD is over the waters;
the God of glory thunders, the LORD, over mighty waters.
The voice of the LORD is powerful;
the voice of the LORD is full of majesty.
The voice of the LORD breaks the cedars;
the LORD breaks the cedars of Lebanon.
He makes Lebanon skip like a calf,
and Sirion like a young wild ox.
The voice of the LORD
flashes forth flames of fire.
The voice of the LORD shakes the wilderness;
the LORD shakes the wilderness of Kadesh.
The voice of the LORD causes the oaks to whirl,
and strips the forest bare; and in his temple all say, "Glory!"
The LORD sits enthroned over the flood;
the LORD sits enthroned as king forever.
May the LORD give strength to his people!
May the LORD bless his people with peace!

SECOND SUNDAY AFTER EPIPHANY

Isaiah 62:1-5　　　　　　　　　　　　　　　　　Psalm 36:5-10
1 Corinthians 12:1-11　　　　　　　　　　　　　　John 2:1-11

• CALL TO WORSHIP
Come, Christians, worship the one who delights in you. You are not forsaken and desolate. You are called by the new name of Jesus Christ.

• PRAYER OF CONFESSION
Faithful God, you have not forsaken us. We have not always been faithful to you. We value your call to virtuous living, but often live at a lower level. We appreciate the fidelity of our friends and spouses, but sometimes betray and abandon them. You give us a variety of gifts to serve you in the church, but much remains undone because we squander the abilities you have given us on less worthy causes. Forgive our erratic service that reflects incomplete obedience, for the sake of your ever-obedient Son, Jesus Christ. Amen.

• DECLARATION OF GOD'S FORGIVENESS
Friends, hear the Good News. Your God rejoices over you as a bridegroom rejoices over the bride. Friends, believe the Good News. In Jesus Christ, we are forgiven.

• EXHORTATION
You all have a variety of gifts, but the same Spirit. There are varieties of service. Let us serve the same God.

• PRAYER OF THE DAY
Divine Winemaker, the wine you give us at your table is more precious than the wine you made at Cana. We are pledged to do whatever you tell us to do, so that with the whole church we may extend your table to the remotest places in human society, and many may come at the last to the wedding feast of the Lamb. Amen.

• PRAYER OF THANKSGIVING
Loving God, you give yourself to all of us, to the young and the innocent, to the jaded and the disenchanted, to the tired and despairing. Your love is like the love of the young bridegroom, like the love of the lonely widower finding a lonely widow, like the love of a king that marries an

unlikely commoner. None can be deserving of your love, but all of us can be grateful and return your love with thankful devotion, like your Son, Jesus Christ. Amen.

• **PRAYER OF DEDICATION**
Supreme Worker, the offerings we bring have been earned in a variety of jobs. It is our intention that all our work should serve your purposes for all your people. Use these gifts to serve many people in many ways; through Jesus Christ our Lord. Amen.

• **PSALM 36:5-10**
Your steadfast love, O LORD, extends to the heavens,
your faithfulness to the clouds.
Your righteousness is like the mighty mountains,
your judgments are like the great deep;
you save humans and animals alike, O LORD.
How precious is your steadfast love, O God!
All people may take refuge in the shadow of your wings.
They feast on the abundance of your house,
and you give them drink from the river of your delights.
For with you is the fountain of life;
in your light we see light.
O continue your steadfast love to those who know you,
and your salvation to the upright of heart!

THIRD SUNDAY AFTER EPIPHANY

Nehemiah 8:1-3,5-6,8-10   Psalm 19
1 Corinthians 12:12-31a   Luke 4:14-21

• CALL TO WORSHIP
You are the body of Christ, member for member. Strive after the better gifts...I will show you a still more excellent way.

• PRAYER OF CONFESSION
Living Designer, you have created the church to be one body with many members working together under the control of the head, Jesus Christ. Forgive us if we have acted toward anyone as if they did not matter, or as if the church could get along without them. Excuse discrimination that gives more praise to some than they deserve at the expense of others who serve modestly without recognition. We do not always share joy and sorrow equally as we are meant to do. Pardon us for the sake of Jesus Christ who forgets no one. Amen.

• DECLARATION OF GOD'S FORGIVENESS
Hear the Good News! One Holy Spirit was poured out for all of us to drink. The weakest of us is still indispensable to the Body of Christ, the Church. Friends, believe the Good News. In Jesus Christ, we are forgiven.

• EXHORTATION
The Spirit of the Lord has been given to you to preach the Good News to the poor, to proclaim liberty to captives and recovery of sight to the blind. Set free the oppressed. Proclaim this year of the Lord's favor.

• PRAYER OF THE DAY
Come alive to us again, living Word, in the hearing of the written Word. Gather us to yourself as we gather to the reading and preaching of the Word so that understanding your will for us, we may go to do it, individually and together. Amen.

• PRAYER OF THANKSGIVING
God-out-of-hiding, speaking and acting, we rejoice in every rediscovery of your written word by the hand of prophets and apostles. We are moved to tears when your voice sounds again in our ears after the silence of

years. We come to the table to feast on the rich food and sweet drink that is provided in the sacrament. We give thanks for the spiritual refreshment and inner strength you give us. Let our joy overflow in invitation to others to join us in our feasting; through Jesus Christ our Lord. Amen.

• **PRAYER OF DEDICATION**
Spirit of the church, enable us to do what needs to be done, whether little or much, that all of us, doing our part, may help to complete your work in the world. Amen.

• **PSALM 19:1-14**
The heavens are telling the glory of God;
and the firmament proclaims his handiwork.
Day to day pours forth speech,
and night to night declares knowledge.
There is no speech, nor are there words;
their voice is not heard;
yet their voice goes out through all the earth,
and their words to the end of the world.
In the heavens he has set a tent for the sun,
which comes out like a bridegroom from his wedding canopy,
and like a strong man runs its course with joy.
Its rising is from the end of the heavens,
and its circuit to the end of them;
and nothing is hid from its heat.
The law of the LORD is perfect, reviving the soul;
the decrees of the LORD are sure, making wise the simple;
the precepts of the LORD are right, rejoicing the heart;
the commandment of the LORD is clear, enlightening the eyes;
the fear of the LORD is pure, enduring forever;
the ordinances of the LORD are true and righteous altogether.
More to be desired are they than gold, even much fine gold;
sweeter also than honey, and drippings of the honeycomb.
Moreover by them is your servant warned;
in keeping them there is great reward.
But who can detect their errors?
Clear me from hidden faults.
Keep back your servant also from the insolent;
do not let them have dominion over me.
Then I shall be blameless,
and innocent of great transgression.
Let the words of my mouth and the meditation of my heart be
acceptable to you, O LORD, my rock and my redeemer.

FOURTH SUNDAY AFTER EPIPHANY

Jeremiah 1:4-10 Psalm 71:1-6
1 Corinthians 13:1-13 Luke 4:21-30

• **CALL TO WORSHIP**
Young and old, give praise to God, who sustains us from childhood to adulthood, through birth and through death.

• **PRAYER OF CONFESSION**
God of all places, familiar and foreign, forgive us if we are open only to the word of the strange prophet and closed to the truth when it comes from a familiar person. Excuse the pride that discounts what our neighbors and friends can do, assuming that only the distant expert could be wiser than ourselves. Pardon the doubt that prevents doing in our place what others have accomplished in other places but in similar circumstances. We are sorry if we have stood in the way of your work, blocking the advance of the church of your beloved Son, Jesus of Nazareth. Amen.

• **DECLARATION OF GOD'S FORGIVENESS**
Hear the Good News! God's love lasts forever. There is no place it cannot reach. There is no age it cannot touch. Friends, believe the Good News. In Jesus Christ, we are forgiven.

• **EXHORTATION**
Make love your quest. Prophets' work will end. The ecstasy of tongues will fade. Some knowledge will lose its usefulness, but there will always be the need for love.

• **PRAYER OF THE DAY**
Divine Speaker, let us hear your gracious words from any lips. Divine Healer, let us feel your healing touch by any hand. Let no spirit of doubt prevent your work through our talents or those of others, in the name of Jesus Christ. Amen.

• **PRAYER OF THANKSGIVING**
God of love, we are grateful for the love you have shown us in Christ and through other persons, for patience with our failings, for kindness in our weak moments, for praise when we have done our best, for forgiveness

without counting the times, for those who go with us when the going gets rough, for those who trust us again after we have abused their trust. For all gifts of love, we thank you, and especially that your love for us is stronger than death. Amen.

• **PRAYER OF DEDICATION**
Loving God, we respond to you with such love as we have. Without our heart's love, our most generous offering, and even martyrdom, would not make us any better. We want to be even more loving, like Jesus Christ. Amen.

• **PSALM 71:1-6**
In you, O LORD, I take refuge;
let me never be put to shame.
In your righteousness deliver me and rescue me;
incline your ear to me and save me.
Be to me a rock of refuge,
a strong fortress, to save me,
for you are my rock and my fortress.
Rescue me, O my God, from the hand of the wicked,
from the grasp of the unjust and cruel.
For you, O Lord, are my hope,
my trust, O LORD, from my youth.
Upon you I have leaned from my birth;
it was you who took me from my mother's womb.
My praise is continually of you.

FIFTH SUNDAY AFTER EPIPHANY

Isaiah 6:1-8 (9-13)   Psalm 138
1 Corinthians 15:1-11   Luke 5:1-11

• CALL TO WORSHIP
For God's love and faithfulness, let us praise God's name. For the promise of God is as wide as the heavens.

• PRAYER OF CONFESSION
God-in-hiding, you catch us unawares. In frightening circumstances, we find ourselves saying: "What did I do to deserve this?" In incredibly good times, we find ourselves saying, "What did I do to deserve this?" Whenever we encounter you unexpectedly, a sense of guilt may catch us and we want you to go away. But we would rather have your forgiveness than your absence, your purging than your rejection. Forgive our sins and prepare us to serve you, through Jesus our Savior. Amen.

• DECLARATION OF GOD'S FORGIVENESS
Hear the Good News! You are saved by the gospel if you hold firmly to it. Friends, believe the Good News. In Jesus Christ, we are forgiven.

• EXHORTATION
Let God's grace be at work in you, drawing others into the fellowship of Christ's church.

• PRAYER OF THE DAY
Urge your service on us, Lord Jesus, that we may be willing to put aside all other priorities in order to follow you. Having received your forgiveness, we accept your assignment. Amen.

• PRAYER OF THANKSGIVING
For visions of your glory, we give thanks, Holy God; for experiences of conversion, we give thanks, Holy Jesus; for confirmation and commissioning, we give thanks, Holy Spirit. For every time and place hallowed by such experiences, we declare our joyful memories. Great is your glory, O God. Our joy in you gives us strength to do your work enabled by your grace in Jesus Christ. Amen.

- **PRAYER OF DEDICATION**
It is by your grace, Lord Jesus, that we are what we are, not all that we yet may be, but wanting to be used by you in the saving work of your church. Amen.

- **PSALM 138**
I give you thanks, O LORD, with my whole heart;
before the gods I sing your praise;
I bow down toward your holy temple and give thanks to your name for your steadfast love and your faithfulness;
for you have exalted your name and your word above everything.
On the day I called, you answered me,
you increased my strength of soul.
All the kings of the earth shall praise you, O LORD,
for they have heard the words of your mouth.
They shall sing of the ways of the LORD,
for great is the glory of the LORD.
For though the LORD is high, he regards the lowly;
but the haughty he perceives from far away.
Though I walk in the midst of trouble, you preserve me against the wrath of my enemies;
you stretch out your hand, and your right hand delivers me.
The LORD will fulfill his purpose for me;
your steadfast love, O LORD, endures forever.
Do not forsake the work of your hands.

SIXTH SUNDAY AFTER EPIPHANY

Jeremiah 17:5-10　　　　　　　　　　　　　　　　　　　　Psalm 1
1 Corinthians 15:12-20　　　　　　　　　　　　　　　　　Luke 6:17-26

- **CALL TO WORSHIP**

Come, put your confidence in God and you will not be disappointed.

- **PRAYER OF CONFESSION**

Despite your warnings through prophets and psalmists, God of truth, we are frequently deceived by the silks and satins of palaces and cathedrals. We misplace our trust when we put our trust in such persons and not in you. You frequently speak through rough and ready persons like John the Baptist, heal the sick through poor people like Jesus of Nazareth, comfort the dying through servants like Mother Teresa of Calcutta. Forgive our admiration of false glories, through Jesus our Savior. Amen.

- **DECLARATION OF GOD'S FORGIVENESS**

Hear the Good News! You are blessed if you do not find Jesus Christ to be a stumbling block, and believe the Good News he preaches to the poor. Friends, believe the Good News. In Jesus Christ, we are forgiven.

- **EXHORTATION**

Beware of the frivolous life. These joys soon disappear. Following Christ may not always be easy, but the rewards are enduring.

- **PRAYER OF THE DAY**

Save us, Son of Man, Child of God, from the casual life without commitment to you and without compassion for the sick and poor of the world. Satisfy us with that which is eternal in you, the ever-living Christ. Amen.

- **PRAYER OF THANKSGIVING**

God of the living, Christ of the Resurrection, eternal Spirit, we rejoice in the survival of the church, giving thanks that the message that Christ has been raised from death has been heard and believed by many, from the time of the apostles to this day. We live in joyful belief that it is not a delusion and that we are not lost in our sins. You have vindicated the Christ in resurrection, and received him into heaven to intercede for us. Glory be to you, O God, now and always. Amen.

- **PRAYER OF DEDICATION**

Though our lives, O God, are not as fruitful as they will be, receive what we are, and what we will become, and whatever we may accomplish, by your grace in Jesus Christ. Amen.

- **PSALM 1**

Happy are those who do not follow the advice of the wicked,
or take the path that sinners tread, or sit in the seat of scoffers;
but their delight is in the law of the LORD,
and on his law they meditate day and night.
They are like trees planted by streams of water,
which yield their fruit in its season,
and their leaves do not wither.
In all that they do, they prosper.
The wicked are not so,
but are like chaff that the wind drives away.
Therefore the wicked will not stand in the judgment,
nor sinners in the congregation of the righteous;
for the LORD watches over the way of the righteous,
but the way of the wicked will perish.

SEVENTH SUNDAY AFTER EPIPHANY

Genesis 45:3-11, 15   Psalm 37:1-11, 39-40
1 Corinthians 15:35-38, 42-50   Luke 6:27-38

• **CALL TO WORSHIP**
Be still in God's presence and worship expectantly. Take delight in prayer, and you will receive your heart's desire.

• **PRAYER OF CONFESSION**
Compassionate Parent, understanding Brother, loving and forgiving Spirit, you know how weak we are and how prone to retaliate when treated spitefully. We would rather return a curse with a curse and a blow with a blow. We refuse many who ask us for what we think we do not owe. We are ready to sue for the return of what is rightfully ours. How is it that you expect us to do good to those who hate us? Is it really possible that we could become so much like Jesus Christ? Forgive us, for his sake, for we are not. Amen.

• **DECLARATION OF GOD'S FORGIVENESS**
Hear the Good News! As we have worn the likeness of the human in the earth, we shall wear the likeness of the heavenly one, the last Adam, Jesus Christ. Friends, believe the Good News! In Jesus Christ, we are forgiven.

• **EXHORTATION**
Do for others just what you want them to do for you.

• **PRAYER OF THE DAY**
How shall we be like you and your royal Son Jesus, heavenly Sovereign, unless you teach us kindness, and a nobility that we rarely practice, not merely respecting our enemies, but actually loving them and praying for them as Jesus did. Amen.

• **PRAYER OF THANKSGIVING**
Life Giver, life Sharer, life Sustainer, many of us have experienced the nearness of death and give thanks for your restorative gifts of healing and health. Especially when life is uncertain, we rejoice in your constant love and in the tender affection of our closest family and friends. When we have been wronged, we are happy again when justice has been

brought about. Most of all we are grateful that you do not treat us as our sins deserve but with measureless forgiveness and mercy. All praise to you whose nature is life, but who in Christ Jesus shared our mortality that we might have the hope of resurrection and eternal life. Amen.

• **PRAYER OF DEDICATION**
Heavenly Monarch, your monarchy can not be possessed by flesh and blood, nor purchased with silver and gold, but we can serve you with all that we are and have as you give us the enabling Spirit through Jesus Christ. Amen.

• **PSALM 37:1-11, 39-40**
Do not fret because of the wicked;
do not be envious of wrongdoers,
for they will soon fade like the grass,
and wither like the green herb.
Trust in the LORD, and do good;
so you will live in the land, and enjoy security.
Take delight in the LORD,
and he will give you the desires of your heart.
Commit your way to the LORD;
trust in him, and he will act.
He will make your vindication shine like the light,
and the justice of your cause like the noonday.
Be still before the LORD,
and wait patiently for him;
do not fret over those who prosper in their way,
over those who carry out evil devices.
Refrain from anger, and forsake wrath.
Do not fret — it leads only to evil.
For the wicked shall be cut off,
but those who wait for the LORD shall inherit the land.
Yet a little while, and the wicked will be no more;
though you look diligently for their place, they will not be there.
But the meek shall inherit the land,
and delight themselves in abundant prosperity.
The salvation of the righteous is from the LORD;
he is their refuge in the time of trouble.
The LORD helps them and rescues them;
*he rescues them from the wicked, and saves them,
because they take refuge in him.*

EIGHTH SUNDAY AFTER EPIPHANY

Isaiah 55:10-13 or Sirach 27:4-7 Psalm 92:1-4, 12-15
1 Corinthians 15:51-58 Luke 6:39-49

• CALL TO WORSHIP
Declare the love of our Sovereign every morning, the constancy of the Most High every night. Let us approach with music and the sounding of chords, for God is majestic in deed and in thought.

• PRAYER OF CONFESSION
God of glory, God of humility, God of truth, how silly our wild blustering must seem to you. We are full of resentment against you in times of trouble and then certain of your absolute fairness and restraint. We are quick to speak and slow to think, quick to teach those we believe to be less learned than ourselves, slow to learn from those with greater experience and wisdom. We can make fine distinctions in the morals of others and miss gross faults in ourselves. Forgive our vacillation and lack of proportion. Hear the pleading of our advocate, Jesus Christ. Amen.

• DECLARATION OF GOD'S FORGIVENESS
Hear the Good News! God gives us the victory over sin and death through Jesus Christ. Friends, believe the Good News. In Jesus Christ, we are forgiven.

• EXHORTATION
Stand firm and immovable and work for Christ always. Work without limit, since you know that what you do in the Spirit cannot be lost.

• PRAYER OF THE DAY
Teach us, wise Tutor, to be quiet when we have nothing good to say. Root out the evil in us so that when we speak, what we say may be the overflowing of love and goodness from the Holy Spirit within us. Amen.

• PRAYER OF THANKSGIVING
How beautiful in your goodness, O God, are many aged worshippers in your house. Their declaration is of your great goodness and no idle boasting of their own religious prowess. Young and old flourish as a garden of trees nourished by your word and luxuriant in virtue and the fruits of the Spirit. We are varied in our strengths but you are the source

of all goodness that we may manifest. All praise to, Planter of gardens, Builder of the Church, Nourisher of souls. Amen.

• **PRAYER OF DEDICATION**
We would worship you, O God, with our best gifts of words and music, with our most intense attention and serious intentions, with our thoughtful contributions and our careful service, in Jesus' name. Amen.

• **PSALM 92:1-4, 12-15**
It is good to give thanks to the LORD,
to sing praises to your name, O Most High;
to declare your steadfast love in the morning,
and your faithfulness by night,
to the music of the lute and the harp,
to the melody of the lyre.
For you, O LORD, have made me glad by your work;
at the works of your hands I sing for joy.
The righteous flourish like the palm tree,
and grow like a cedar in Lebanon.
They are planted in the house of the LORD;
they flourish in the courts of our God.
In old age they still produce fruit;
they are always green and full of sap,
showing that the LORD is upright;
he is my rock, and there is no unrighteousness in him.

NINTH SUNDAY AFTER EPIPHANY

1 Kings 8:22-23,41-43　　　　　　　　　　　　Psalm 96:1-9
Galatians 1:1-12　　　　　　　　　　　　　　　　Luke 7:1-10

• **CALL TO WORSHIP**
Worship the Eternal One in holy splendor; Honor and majesty are expressed to God. Strength and beauty belong to God's church. From day to day tell of the salvation of our God.

• **PRAYER OF CONFESSION**
God of truth, Christ the truth, Spirit of truth, forgive us if we treat casually the written word handed down to us by the apostles and translators in the church. You have communicated with us in every generation seeking to widen our reception of the larger truth. We can sometimes overvalue our own ideas and not test them with the ideals of Jesus in word and deed. Pardon our passions for novelty and what is pleasant but not true; through Jesus Christ who is our way, our truth, our life. Amen.

• **DECLARATION OF GOD'S FORGIVENESS**
Hear the Good News! Our Savior, Jesus Christ, gave himself for our sins to set us free from the present evil age, according to the will of our God and Father. Friends, believe the Good News. In Jesus Christ, we are forgiven.

• **EXHORTATION**
Hold fast to this Good News and do not be led astray by any false gospel.

• **PRAYER OF THE DAY**
Make us ambassadors of good will, O Christ, that we may encourage those who want your help and healing to come to you, confident of your openness and your loving acceptance of strangers. Amen.

• **PRAYER OF THANKSGIVING**
We give thanks to you, Eternal God, for there is no other God like you in heaven above or on earth beneath. Though heaven is your dwelling place you have also come among us in Jesus Christ. Whether in buildings made with hands or without them you have a habitation for the Spirit in the lives of all who acknowledge Jesus to be the Lord. We will sing your praise

and honor your name in every house of prayer for you are one God for one people, your people. Amen.

• **PRAYER OF DEDICATION**
God of the church, you keep covenant with your people and steadfast love for your servants who walk before you with all their heart. Receive the offerings we bring in support of this house of prayer that all the people of this community may know your name and worship you, through Jesus Christ our Lord. Amen.

• **PSALM 96:1-9**
O sing to the LORD a new song;
sing to the LORD, all the earth.
Sing to the LORD, bless his name;
tell of his salvation from day to day.
Declare his glory among the nations,
his marvelous works among all the peoples.
For great is the LORD, and greatly to be praised;
he is to be revered above all gods.
For all the gods of the peoples are idols,
but the LORD made the heavens.
Honor and majesty are before him;
strength and beauty are in his sanctuary.
Ascribe to the LORD, O families of the peoples,
ascribe to the LORD glory and strength.
Ascribe to the LORD the glory due his name;
bring an offering, and come into his courts.
Worship the LORD in holy splendor;
tremble before him, all the earth.

LAST SUNDAY AFTER EPIPHANY
Transfiguration

Exodus 34:29-35   Psalm 99
2 Corinthians 3:12-4:2   Luke 9:28-36

• CALL TO WORSHIP
Join in the praise of the majestic name for our mighty Sovereign is supreme over all nations. Worship with reverence before God's throne, for God is holy.

• PRAYER OF CONFESSION
God of glory, God of grace, God to be seen in human face, we are not worthy of the vision of your glory and are not pure in heart so as to glimpse your holiness without shame. We are able to see you now as through a dark glass but anticipate the day when we will be ready to see you face to face. Extend your patience with us as we learn to love you fully and our neighbor as ourselves, through Jesus our Savior. Amen.

• DECLARATION OF GOD'S FORGIVENESS
Hear the Good News! Though our sins are punishable, God forgives us as we confess our sins. Friends, believe the Good News. In Jesus Christ, we are forgiven.

• EXHORTATION:
In the full light of truth live in God's sight and try to commend yourselves to everyone's good conscience.

• PRAYER OF THE DAY
Revealing God, we would hear your word again so that, more brilliantly than any other memorable human beings, we enjoy the perception of Jesus as having the qualities that are those of your chosen. Amen.

• PRAYER OF THANKSGIVING
God of Moses and Elijah, Peter and Paul, Luther and Calvin, Pope John the Twenty-third and Billy Graham, we give thanks for all who have revealed your word by preaching and writing. David and Luke, Bach and Mendelssohn, Keble and Fannie Crosby, we rejoice in the music and song that has been a means of expressing our praise to your name. God of Michelangelo and Rembrandt, Salvatore Dali and Frances Hook, we

appreciate the art that has brightened our vision of your glory. Most of all we celebrate the grace you have manifest in Jesus Christ himself, seen by his generation and remembered ever since in word and sacrament. Amen.

• PRAYER OF DEDICATION
God of Clouds and streaming Light, wake us from dozing discipleship to alert witnessing and the devotion of what we are and what we have to the needs of the world in our time. Amen.

• PSALM 99
The LORD is king; let the peoples tremble!
He sits enthroned upon the cherubim; let the earth quake!
The LORD is great in Zion;
he is exalted over all the peoples.
Let them praise your great and awesome name.
Holy is he!
Mighty King, lover of justice, you have established equity;
you have executed justice and righteousness in Jacob.
Extol the LORD our God;
worship at his footstool. Holy is he!
Moses and Aaron were among his priests,
Samuel also was among those who called on his name.
They cried to the LORD, and he answered them.
He spoke to them in the pillar of cloud;
they kept his decrees,
and the statutes that he gave them.
O LORD our God, you answered them;
you were a forgiving God to them,
but an avenger of their wrongdoings.
Extol the LORD our God,
and worship at his holy mountain;
for the LORD our God is holy.

ASH WEDNESDAY

Joel 2:1-2,12-17a or Isaiah 58:1-12　　　　　　　Psalm 51:1-17
2 Corinthians 5:20b—6:10　　　　　　　　　Matthew 6:1-6, 16-21

• **CALL TO WORSHIP**
Take joy in your salvation and be willing to obey God as the Spirit prompts you.

• **PRAYER OF CONFESSION**
God above all, you have created us from the ground up and in Christ came to our turf, to show us again that the earth is yours and you have made all things to be good. Your own Spirit infused life into the lifeless so that the human race should be distinct not in its physical properties but in its ability to control behavior individually and socially. Forgive our lack of self-control and our abuse of what you have created for the good of all. May such fasting and penitence as we may practice enable us to balance things out and to bring the spiritual and the physical into equilibrium, following the example of Jesus Christ. Amen.

• **DECLARATION OF GOD'S FORGIVENESS**
Hear the Good News! God appointed the sinless Christ to share our sin in order that in union with him we might share the goodness of God. Friends, believe the Good News. In Jesus Christ, we are forgiven.

• **EXHORTATION**
Having received God's grace in Christ, do not let it be wasted, but express it to others enriching them as well.

• **PRAYER OF THE DAY**
Distinguished and distinguishing Spirit, grant us wisdom, so that both our fasting and our charitable actions are inconspicuous. Then only you will know what we have done and we will be content with your private reward. Amen.

• **PRAYER OF THANKSGIVING**
Maker, Sharer, and Shaper of the human Spirit, we are thankful that we have not been cast in stone that cannot be reshaped. You forgive our failures and give us further opportunities to restore some of the beauty of your image. We can be thankful even for the trouble and suffering that

brings us closer to you in prayer. Then at least we may recognize our need to depend on you. We welcome this Lenten season as a time of personal renewal. Amen

• **PRAYER OF DEDICATION**
Eternal God, Ruler of time and space, we offer to you an expanded portion of our time and increased concentration of our attention during this Lenten season for our own growth in grace and in love for your family. Amen

• **PSALM 51:1-17**
Have mercy on me, O God, according to your steadfast love;
according to your abundant mercy blot out my transgressions.
Wash me thoroughly from my iniquity,
and cleanse me from my sin.
For I know my transgressions,
and my sin is ever before me.
Against you, you alone, have I sinned,
and done what is evil in your sight,
so that you are justified in your sentence
and blameless when you pass judgment.
Indeed, I was born guilty,
a sinner when my mother conceived me.
You desire truth in the inward being;
therefore teach me wisdom in my secret heart.
Purge me with hyssop, and I shall be clean;
wash me, and I shall be whiter than snow.
Let me hear joy and gladness;
let the bones that you have crushed rejoice.
Hide your face from my sins,
and blot out all my iniquities.
Create in me a clean heart, O God,
and put a new and right spirit within me.
Do not cast me away from your presence,
and do not take your holy spirit from me.
Restore to me the joy of your salvation,
and sustain in me a willing spirit.

FIRST SUNDAY IN LENT

Deuteronomy 26:1-11   Psalm 91:1-2, 9-16
Romans 10:8b-13   Luke 4:1-13

• CALL TO WORSHIP
Hear what God's word says: I will save those who love me. When they call to me, I will answer them; when they are in trouble, I will be with them.

• PRAYER OF CONFESSION
Your name, O God, is to be spoken with reverence and hope. We have spoken it irreverently at times and not at all when we might have called upon you with expectation of your presence and help. We know you are present but put you out of our minds when we worship wealth and power. Most of us would not acknowledge ourselves devil worshippers and yet succumb to temptations that Jesus resisted with the strength of your Word. Forgive our lack of faith in your saving power wanting to be saved only from the consequences of our sins and not from the sins through Jesus Christ our Lord. Amen.

• DECLARATION OF GOD'S FORGIVENESS
Hear the Good News! Everyone who calls out to the Lord for help will be saved. Friends, believe the Good News! In Jesus Christ, we are forgiven.

• EXHORTATION
Confess that Jesus is Lord. Believe that God raised him from the dead. It is by our confession that we are saved.

• PRAYER OF THE DAY
God our strength, in times of need, save us from despair. In times of indecision, save us from opting for power rather than service. In times of danger, save us from hiding rather than risking what we may do with your approval and help. We would be more like your Son, Jesus. Amen.

• PRAYER OF THANKSGIVING
God above history, God in our history, God at the end of our history, as the ancestors of Israel were wandering Aramaeans, so our ancestors were emigrating pilgrims, seeking freedom to worship and to govern

themselves according to an enlightened conscience. We are grateful for their pioneering. For all the freedoms we enjoy in this land of immigrants we give you our thanks, remembering also that we live among the remnants of those who lived here before us. We give thanks for their love of the land the forests and the creatures which you have created. Help us to show our thanksgiving in the continual re-examination of conscience that we may live justly, show mercy, and walk in humility before you, like Jesus Christ, your Son, our Lord. Amen.

• **PRAYER OF DEDICATION**
As your people Israel, worshipped you in the presentation of the first part of the harvest, so may we your people of Christ's church, worship you in the presentation of our offerings, remembering also the ministers, and those of the poor in this and every land who look to us for the gifts that we share, through Jesus Christ our Lord. Amen.

• **PSALM 91:1-2, 9-16**
You who live in the shelter of the Most High,
who abide in the shadow of the Almighty,
will say to the LORD, "My refuge and my fortress;
my God, in whom I trust."
Because you have made the LORD your refuge,
the Most High your dwelling place,
no evil shall befall you,
no scourge come near your tent.
For he will command his angels concerning you
to guard you in all your ways.
On their hands they will bear you up,
so that you will not dash your foot against a stone.
You will tread on the lion and the adder,
the young lion and the serpent you will trample under foot.
Those who love me, I will deliver;
I will protect those who know my name.
When they call to me, I will answer them;
I will be with them in trouble, I will rescue them and honor them.
With long life I will satisfy them,
and show them my salvation.

SECOND SUNDAY IN LENT

Genesis 15:1-12, 17, 18   Psalm 27
Philippians 3:17-4:1   Luke 13:31-35 or Luke 9:28-36

• **CALL TO WORSHIP**
Come seek God's face...Wait for the Lord... Take courage... Be strong.

• **PRAYER OF CONFESSION**
Creating Spirit, hear our confession. We are often forgetful of who we are and in whose likeness we are created. We regret the imbalance in our lives that too often allows our appetites to run away with us, so that we seem to live for eating and drinking and love-making. Our minds are too busy with plans to get ahead and satisfy bodily desires to the exclusion of the refreshment of the spirit, the exercise of the mind, the discipline of the body. Forgive our excesses and deliver us from them through our Lord Jesus Christ. Amen.

• **DECLARATION OF GOD'S FORGIVENESS**
Hear the Good News! Christ will transfigure these bodies belonging to our humble state, and give them a form like that of his own resplendent body by the very power which enables him to make all things subject to himself. Friends, believe the Good News. In Jesus Christ, we are forgiven.

• **EXHORTATION**
Live as citizens of heaven. Stand firm in the faith. Look to Jesus who will bring us joy and a crown beyond the cross.

• **PRAYER OF THE DAY**
God of order and truth, among the many persons who appear heroic to us, help us to look only to those who remind us most vividly of Jesus of Nazareth. Help us to heed only those whose advice and guidance lead us in his ways. Speak to us through whom you please but let us never turn away from your eternal Son. Amen.

• **PRAYER OF THANKSGIVING**
Eternal God, who in Jesus Christ accepted the limitations of time as a pioneer of perseverance, we thank you for the promise that waits beyond the years of waiting, for the transformation and transfiguration that lies

beyond the days of human frailty and suffering, for the light that breaks through dark clouds, and the glory that outshines all humiliation. We are grateful for the life and suffering of Jesus and rejoice in the glory that now is his and which one day he will share with all who are willing to share his suffering; through the same Jesus Christ your Son and our Intercessor. Amen.

• PRAYER OF DEDICATION
In themselves our gifts are lifeless, living God, but they are a portion of our livelihood. Accept these offerings of obedient service in honor of your name and for the benefit of our neighbors in the world; through Jesus Christ our Lord. Amen.

• PSALM 27
The LORD is my light and my salvation; whom shall I fear?
The LORD is the stronghold of my life; of whom shall I be afraid?
When evildoers assail me to devour my flesh —
my adversaries and foes — they shall stumble and fall.
Though an army encamp against me, my heart shall not fear;
though war rise up against me, yet I will be confident.
One thing I asked of the LORD, that will I seek after:
to live in the house of the LORD all the days of my life,
to behold the beauty of the LORD, and to inquire in his temple.
For he will hide me in his shelter in the day of trouble;
he will conceal me under the cover of his tent;
he will set me high on a rock.
Now my head is lifted up above my enemies all around me,
and I will offer in his tent sacrifices with shouts of joy;
I will sing and make melody to the LORD.
Hear, O LORD, when I cry aloud,
be gracious to me and answer me!
"Come," my heart says, "seek his face!"
Your face, LORD, do I seek.
Do not hide your face from me.
Do not turn your servant away in anger,
you who have been my help.
Do not cast me off, do not forsake me, O God of my salvation!
If my father and mother forsake me, the LORD will take me up.
Teach me your way, O LORD,
and lead me on a level path because of my enemies.

Do not give me up to the will of my adversaries,
for false witnesses have risen against me,
and they are breathing out violence.
I believe that I shall see the goodness of the LORD in the land of the living. Wait for the LORD; be strong, *and let your heart take courage; wait for the LORD!*

THIRD SUNDAY IN LENT

Isaiah 55:1-9　　　　　　　　　　　　　　　　Psalm 63:1-8
1 Corinthians 10:1-13　　　　　　　　　　　　Luke 13:1-9

• **CALL TO WORSHIP** (Responsively)
Seek the Eternal One who may be found.
Call upon God while the Spirit is near;
forsake wicked ways, and unrighteous thoughts;
return to the Eternal One, who will have mercy on you,
and to our God, who will abundantly pardon.

• **PRAYER OF CONFESSION**
Holy God, how exalted are your ways! Holy Savior, how sinless is your life! Holy Spirit, how pure is your nature! Whatever progress we have made along the road of righteousness we are far behind the advance of your Son Jesus. Continue to call us back when we go off on a tangent and recall us to the upward way for we would more nearly follow Jesus Christ. Amen.

• **DECLARATION OF GOD'S FORGIVENESS**
Hear the Good News! God comes to free us from slavery to every passion. Friends, believe the Good News! In Jesus Christ, we are forgiven.

• **EXHORTATION**
Repent. God is patient but looks for the fruits of repentance.

• **PRAYER OF THE DAY**
Save us, God of the living, from any misconception that because we survive and others meet untimely death, that we are more virtuous than they. Whether our lives are long or short may they be truly fruitful through the Spirit of Jesus Christ. Amen.

• **PRAYER OF THANKSGIVING**
God of order, God of compassion, God of love, we rejoice that catastrophes are as infrequent as they are. Even then you inspire mutual helpfulness among those who suffer from them as well as those near enough to lend a hand. We are grateful that we have learned how to avoid some of the violence that is part of nature and we are committed to caring for your

creation with all the wisdom you will give us in experience. We praise your wisdom, power, and glory through Jesus Christ our Lord. Amen

• PRAYER OF DEDICATION
Receive the offerings we bring, O God, and sanctify them to the holy purpose of proffering your spiritual gifts to all who desire them; through Jesus Christ our Lord. Amen

• PSALM 63:1-8
O God, you are my God, I seek you,
my soul thirsts for you;
my flesh faints for you,
as in a dry and weary land where there is no water.
So I have looked upon you in the sanctuary,
beholding your power and glory.
Because your steadfast love is better than life,
my lips will praise you.
So I will bless you as long as I live;
I will lift up my hands and call on your name.
My soul is satisfied as with a rich feast,
and my mouth praises you with joyful lips
when I think of you on my bed,
and meditate on you in the watches of the night;
for you have been my help,
and in the shadow of your wings I sing for joy.
My soul clings to you;
your right hand upholds me.

FOURTH SUNDAY IN LENT

Joshua 5:9-12   Psalm 32
2 Corinthians 5:16-21   Luke 15:1-3, 11b-32

• CALL TO WORSHIP
Be glad in the LORD and rejoice, O righteous, and shout for joy, all you upright in heart.

• PRAYER OF CONFESSION
Generous and forgiving Parent, we are not sinless like your Son, Jesus of Nazareth. We confess our misdeeds knowing that you have reconciled us to yourself through the identification of the sinless one with us in our sinfulness. Though we are not worthy to be called your children and deserve to be treated only as servants of earlier times, we come with confidence in your generosity. If we continue in sin, presuming on your forgiveness, mercifully withhold the judgment we have coming to us, for the sake of Jesus Christ. Amen.

• DECLARATION OF GOD'S FORGIVENESS
Hear the Good News! When anyone is united to Christ, there is a new world. The old order has gone, and a new order has already begun. Friends, believe the Good News! In Jesus Christ, we are forgiven.

• EXHORTATION
Celebrate with God the return of every lost and wandering child who returns to the way and to the family of God.

• PRAYER OF THE DAY
Gracious Parent, fill our hearts with such true appreciation of your grace from day to day, that we may avoid self-righteousness and join in the joyful celebration of the recovery and return of other prodigals through Jesus Christ, who came to seek and to save all who are lost. Amen.

• PRAYER OF THANKSGIVING
Though we might well hang our heads in shame, Heavenly Parent, when we remember what we have done contrary to your instruction, we come with joy and shining faces, for you put our past behind us and lead us to a new life of freedom and mutual service. We will bless your name

continually and tell of your goodness to the humble, who will hear and also be glad. With all who have been freed from bondage we celebrate the passover of gladness and the joyful feast of the people of God. All praise be given to you, Holy Parent, Innocent Kin, Family Spirit. Amen.

- **PRAYER OF DEDICATION**

You give us more than we deserve, Divine Provider. What we give is not all that we have, but we are determined to do our share in the work of your family, the Church. Amen.

- **PSALM 32:1-11**

Happy are those whose transgression is forgiven,
whose sin is covered.
Happy are those to whom the LORD imputes no iniquity,
and in whose spirit there is no deceit.
While I kept silence, my body wasted away through my groaning
all day long.
For day and night your hand was heavy upon me;
my strength was dried up as by the heat of summer.
Then I acknowledged my sin to you,
and I did not hide my iniquity;
I said, "I will confess my transgressions to the LORD,"
and you forgave the guilt of my sin.
Therefore let all who are faithful offer prayer to you;
at a time of distress, the rush of mighty waters shall not reach them.
You are a hiding place for me; you preserve me from trouble;
you surround me with glad cries of deliverance.
I will instruct you and teach you the way you should go;
I will counsel you with my eye upon you.
Do not be like a horse or a mule, without understanding,
whose temper must be curbed with bit and bridle,
 else it will not stay near you.
Many are the torments of the wicked,
but steadfast love surrounds those who trust in the LORD.
Be glad in the LORD and rejoice, O righteous,
and shout for joy, all you upright in heart.

FIFTH SUNDAY IN LENT

Isaiah 43:16-21 　　　　　　　　　　　　　　　　　Psalm 126
Philippians 3:4b-14 　　　　　　　　　　　　　　　John 12:1-8

• **CALL TO WORSHIP**
Cease dwelling on days gone by and brooding over past history. Worship in expectation that God will do new things and that now they may break from the bud into flowers and fruit.

• **PRAYER OF CONFESSION**
God for all seasons, we confess that we would rather live in the glorious days of the past than risk the uncertain outcome of the future. We would rather leap ahead to the day of resurrection than undergo our share of the sufferings of Christ. Forgive our zeal for honors and our reluctance to accept either unnoticed service or too conspicuous suffering, through Jesus Christ, who through humiliation came to exaltation. Amen.

• **DECLARATION OF GOD'S FORGIVENESS**
Hear the Good News! With the twelve we are invited to eat and drink at our Lord's Table in the kingdom of God. Friends, believe the Good News! In Jesus Christ, we are forgiven.

• **EXHORTATION**
Forget what is behind and press on to the goal. There you will win the prize, which is God's call to the life above with Christ Jesus.

• **PRAYER OF THE DAY**
Suffering Servant, triumphant Lord, strengthen our resolve to serve you faithfully at the humblest tasks so that we may be prepared for whatever duties you will assign us in the kingdom yet to come, through the power of your resurrection. Amen.

• **PRAYER OF THANKSGIVING**
We bless you, O Lord, for you have heard our cries for mercy. You are our strength and shield and we trust you with all our hearts. You sustain us and our hearts leap up for joy. We praise you with our whole bodies. You are the strength of your people. Without you we cannot hope to complete the race and win the prize. We rejoice in your promised presence with us, now and always. Amen.

• **PRAYER OF DEDICATION**
Receive the faithful service of your church, risen Lord, as we maintain your table and celebrate your supper here in anticipation of the final fulfillment of this passover in the kingdom of God. Amen.

• **PSALM 126** (**Begun in unison**)
(All)When the LORD restored the fortunes of Zion, we were like those who dream.
Then our mouth was filled with laughter,
and our tongue with shouts of joy;
then it was said among the nations,
"The LORD has done great things for them."
The LORD has done great things for us, and we rejoiced.
Restore our fortunes, O LORD, like the watercourses in the Negeb.
May those who sow in tears reap with shouts of joy.
Those who go out weeping, bearing the seed for sowing,
shall come home with shouts of joy, carrying their sheaves.

SIXTH SUNDAY IN LENT
+ As Palm Sunday +++ As Passion Sunday

Isaiah 50:4-9a + Psalm 118:1-2, 19-29
+++ Psalm 31:9-16
Philippians 2:5-11 + Luke 19:28-40
+++ Luke 22:14-23:56 or Luke 23:1-49

• + CALL TO WORSHIP
Reverence the name of the Lord in the evening and his glory to the rising of the sun.

• +++ CALL TO WORSHIP
Morning by morning God wakens us—wakens us to listen as those who are taught. Listen again for the Word of God.

• + PRAYER OF CONFESSION
God of justice, you still look for those who love justice and practice honesty in business and in court. Too often you look in vain for those who will intervene in opposition to injustice and those who will tell the truth without any equivocation. Too often we are cowardly and turn our backs on those who need our advocacy in the cause of freedom with justice. Forgive any compromise of integrity and any indifference to miscarriages of justice. Have mercy on us for the sake of Jesus Christ, your suffering servant and our Savior. Amen.

• +++ PRAYER OF CONFESSION
Sympathetic Parent, Suffering Servant, Consoling Spirit, forgive our apathy in the face of your identification with our sins. We are still so insensitive to the abhorrence you have to all evil. Despite your holiness you forgive our sins both deliberate and unknowing. Hear us as in the silence we bring to mind our more obvious sins... Only in the name of Jesus do we have assurance of pardon and any disposition to examine ourselves more deeply...

• + DECLARATION OF GOD'S FORGIVENESS
Hear the Good News. When it is the Lord GOD who helps you; who will declare you guilty? Friends, believe the good news. In Jesus Christ, we are forgiven.

• + EXHORTATION
Deal mercifully with others, displaying the patience God can give. Be typical of all who in the future will also have faith in Christ and gain eternal life.

• +++ DECLARATION OF GOD'S FORGIVENESS
Hear the words of Jesus even now being said for us: "Father, forgive them for they know not what they do." Friends, believe the Gospel. In Jesus Christ, we are forgiven.

• +++ EXHORTATION
In life and in death commit your lives into the hands of God.

• + PRAYER OF THE DAY
Modest King, receive our praise for all that you do for us from day to day. Save us from silence that sees and receives the gifts of your grace without acknowledgment. We would speak and sing in harmony with all of nature that glorifies you, God of grace. Amen.

• +++ PRAYER OF THE DAY
Sensitizing Spirit, open our hearts to the suffering that our sins add to the suffering of God's chosen One, so that we may be deterred from displeasing our heavenly Parent and desire the purity of holy childhood. Amen.

• + PRAYER OF THANKSGIVING
We rejoice, O God, in your steadfastness. When life is uncertain, you are a rock of refuge. When friends are ashamed of us, you are still merciful and forgiving. How abundant is your goodness beyond all deserving! Your look of love and encouragement we see in the face of Jesus Christ. You see us through places of affliction and set our feet again in a safe place. We praise your name, Creator, Healer, Sustainer. Amen.

• +++ PRAYER OF THANKSGIVING
Loving God, Crucified Christ, Living Spirit, to what lengths you go to manifest your caring for sinners, that Jesus should be counted a criminal to be identified with us all! To what depths, you have come from the majesty of heaven to servitude and suffering, humility and mortality! We rejoice in the glory that now you share again Risen Messiah, having borne our sorrow, you have entered into joy. We live in thankful

expectation of sharing that eternal happiness because of your indescribable self-sacrifice. We give thanks to you, Giver of all good gifts. We give thanks to you, God-given Jesus. We give thanks to you, still given Spirit. Amen.

• +PRAYER OF DEDICATION
Source of all goodness, the temporal value of the offerings we bring varies with the marketplace, but the eternal value of your church's work remains constant as you enable us to serve you in the power of the Spirit. Evermore give us abounding grace through Jesus Christ our Lord. Amen.

• +++ PRAYER OF DEDICATION
No gift of ours can match the gift you have given us in Christ, giving God, but our offerings are an expression of our need to serve you, faithfully and humbly. Amen.

• + PSALM 118:1-2,19-29
O give thanks to the LORD, for he is good;
his steadfast love endures forever!
Let Israel say, "His steadfast love endures forever." Open to me the gates of righteousness,
that I may enter through them and give thanks to the LORD.
This is the gate of the LORD;
the righteous shall enter through it.
I thank you that you have answered me
and have become my salvation.
(All) The stone that the builders rejected has become the chief cornerstone.
This is the LORD's doing;
it is marvelous in our eyes.
This is the day that the LORD has made;
let us rejoice and be glad in it.
Save us, we beseech you, O LORD!
O LORD, we beseech you, give us success!
Blessed is the one who comes in the name of the LORD.
We bless you from the house of the LORD.
The LORD is God, and he has given us light.
Bind the festal procession with branches, up to the horns of the altar.
You are my God, and I will give thanks to you;

you are my God, I will extol you.
O give thanks to the LORD, for he is good,
for his steadfast love endures forever.

• +++ PSALM 31:9-16
Be gracious to me, O LORD, for I am in distress;
my eye wastes away from grief, my soul and body also.
For my life is spent with sorrow,
and my years with sighing;
my strength fails because of my misery,
and my bones waste away.
I am the scorn of all my adversaries,
a horror to my neighbors,
an object of dread to my acquaintances;
those who see me in the street flee from me.
I have passed out of mind like one who is dead;
I have become like a broken vessel.
For I hear the whispering of many—terror all around!
—as they scheme together against me, as they plot to take my life.
But I trust in you, O LORD;
I say, "You are my God."
My times are in your hand;
deliver me from the hand of my enemies and persecutors.
Let your face shine upon your servant;
save me in your steadfast love.

MAUNDY THURSDAY
(Tenebrae Service Using Only Lukan Passages)

([X] identifies the place in the reading where each of seven lights or candles is extinguished)

DARK NIGHT OF BETRAYAL

Opening Hymn: A hymn describing the entry into Jerusalem of Jesus on the donkey.

1. TRIUMPH AND TEARS   Luke 19:28-44
First three verses of the Scottish Paraphrase by William Robertson of Isaiah 53. Tune: St. Mary, C.M.

Fair as a beauteous tender flower
  Amidst the desert grow,
So slighted by a rebel race
  The heavenly Savior rose.

Rejected and despised of men,
  Behold a man of woe!
Grief was his close companion still
  Through all his life below.

Yet all the griefs He felt were ours,
  Ours were the woes He bore:
Pangs, not his own, His spotless soul
  With bitter anguish tore.

Or When Jesus Wept by Wm. Billings verses 1 & 2.

2. TYRANNICAL TENANTS   Luke 19:45-48, 20:1-21
    HYMN: This Is My Father's World, verse 3

3. THEOLOGICAL TESTS AND TEACHING   Luke 20:22-47,
                                                           21:(1-36) 37-38
    HYMN: The God Of Abraham Praise, verses 1 & 2

4. THE TWELVE AND THE TEMPLE POLICE   Luke 22:1-13
   [X1] vs. 6 Plotting to betray Jesus
   HYMN: When We Are Tempted To Deny Your Son,
      by David W. Romig

5. THE TABLE OF THANKSGIVING   Luke 22:14-38
   [X2] vs. 23 Predicting the Betrayal
   HYMN: Here, O Our Lord, We See You Face To Face,
      by Horatius Bonar

THE LAST SUPPER MAY BE CELEBRATED

6. THE TITANIC TEST   Luke 22:39-53
   [X3] vs. 47 Perpetrating the betrayal
   HYMN: Go To Dark Gethsemane,
      by James Montgomery

7. TRIAL BY THE FIRE   Luke 22:54-65
   [X4] vs. 63 Prevaricating Peter
   HYMN: In The Hour Of Trial

8. TRIALS BY COUNCIL, PILATE AND   Luke 22:66—23:12
   HEROD
   [X5] 23:11 Parody of Royalty
   HYMN: O Sacred Head Sore Wounded

9. THE TRADE: JESUS FOR BARABBAS   Luke 23:13-25
   [X6] 23:25 Prisoners Exchanged
   HYMN: Amazing Grace

10. THE GREEN TREE AND THE DRY   Luke 23:26-48
    [X7] 23:44 Paradise Is Promised Where It Was Lost
    SPIRITUAL: Were You There When They Crucified My Lord?

THE BENEDICTION AND QUIET DEPARTURE

EASTER

Acts 10:34-43 Psalm 118:1-2, 14-24
(or Isaiah 65:17-25)
1 Corinthians 15:19-26 John 20:1-18 (Luke 24:1-12)
(or Acts 10:34-43)

• CALL TO WORSHIP
This is the day of the Lord's victory. Let us celebrate and be happy.

• PRAYER OF CONFESSION
God without favorites, we confess that we have our preferences according to nationality and custom. We do not easily accept religious practices other than our own. We find it difficult to discern the similarities below the surface differences and the deeper reverence for you that we may share. We need to learn to witness to our faith in you without pride of race and nationality. Forgive any exclusive attitude that may prevent our communicating the good news of the resurrection of our dying, rising living Savior, Jesus Christ. Amen.

• DECLARATION OF GOD'S FORGIVENESS
Hear the Good News! The Lord's love endures forever. The Lord chastens us but does not surrender us to death. He is our deliverer. Friends, believe the Good News. In Jesus Christ, we are forgiven.

• EXHORTATION
Like Mary Magdalene, go to tell the family of Jesus that he is risen and ascends to his God and ours.

• PRAYER OF THE DAY
Eternal God, grant us time to discover in our own experience the meaning of your written word so that the One who is your word spelled out in our humanity will inform our minds and transform our personalities in the Spirit of Jesus Christ. Amen.

• PRAYER OF THANKSGIVING
You are no grim reaper, Creator of life and Sovereign of death, but a joyful Harvester. We rejoice in the resurrection of Jesus who is the firstfruits of the harvest of the dead. We may live in happy anticipation of our own life beyond death, assured that as in Adam all die so in Christ

all will be brought to life again in your time and place. Thanks to you, our Creator, our Restorer, our Life. Amen.

• **PRAYER OF DEDICATION**
God of the living, not only in one great hour of sharing, but in all the days of our lives, use us and our total resources to help feed the hungry, to heal the sick, to bring good news to the despondent, through Jesus Christ, our risen Lord. Amen.

• **PSALM 118:1-2, 14-24**
O give thanks to the LORD, for he is good;
his steadfast love endures forever!
Let Israel say, "His steadfast love endures forever."
The LORD is my strength and my might;
he has become my salvation.
There are glad songs of victory in the tents of the righteous:
"The right hand of the LORD does valiantly;
the right hand of the LORD is exalted;
the right hand of the LORD does valiantly."
I shall not die,
but I shall live, and recount the deeds of the LORD.
The LORD has punished me severely,
but he did not give me over to death.
Open to me the gates of righteousness,
that I may enter through them and give thanks to the LORD.
This is the gate of the LORD;
the righteous shall enter through it.
I thank you that you have answered me
and have become my salvation.
[All] The stone that the builders rejected has become the chief cornerstone.
This is the LORD's doing; it is marvelous in our eyes.
This is the day that the LORD has made; let us rejoice and be glad in it.

SECOND SUNDAY OF EASTER

Acts 5:27-32　　　　　　　　　　Psalm 118:14-29 or Psalm 150
Revelation 1:4-8　　　　　　　　　　　　　　　　John 20:19-31

• **CALL TO WORSHIP**
Worship reverently the One who is, who was and who is to come, Sovereign of sovereigns, together with the faithful witness, the first-born from the dead, Jesus, our high priest.

• **PRAYER OF CONFESSION**
Alpha God, Omega God, you are our beginning and our end. We confess that we are reluctant to be counted among those responsible for the crucifixion of the one you sent to be our Savior. We may be doubtful too about the testimony to his resurrection. Forgive the pride that prevents our honest confession of sin and the doubt that refuses to hear and see what might strengthen our wavering faith. Despite our reservations, we pray in the name of your special Son, Jesus of Nazareth, your anointed One, our Savior. Amen.

• **DECLARATION OF GOD'S FORGIVENESS**
Hear the Good News! Jesus is alive, and holds the keys of death and death's domain. He is the first and the last and is the living one. He is forgiving and says: Do not be afraid. Friends, believe the Good News! In Jesus Christ, we are forgiven.

• **EXHORTATION**
Exult in the triumph of Jesus over death. He makes us a royal priesthood to bring others to God.

• **PRAYER OF THE DAY**
Come to us, immortal Monarch, in the time of our doubting to reassure us, that as you were vulnerable but victors in the circumstances of history you will bring us safely through all testing to final triumph. Amen.

• **PRAYER OF THANKSGIVING**
Living Spirit, we give thanks for all that has been recorded in the gospels of all that Jesus performed in the presence of the apostles. We rejoice in the other signs too numerous to be written that Christ has given among your people, then and now: the healing of the sick, the peace that has

been given to those who have been doubtful but wanting to believe. We exult in the fellowship of the risen Monarch and live in hope of the final triumph of your rule. Amen.

• **PRAYER OF DEDICATION**
We offer to you, O God, these tangible gifts, daily work, the hymns that we sing, the music that we make, the deeds of kindness done for others, the words of encouragement spoken in your name. Receive and sanctify our gifts to extend the power of your realm to the glory of Jesus Christ, your resurrected Son. Amen.

• **PSALM 118:14-29**
The LORD is my strength and my might;
he has become my salvation.
There are glad songs of victory in the tents of the righteous:
"The right hand of the LORD does valiantly;
the right hand of the LORD is exalted;
the right hand of the LORD does valiantly."
I shall not die, but I shall live,
and recount the deeds of the LORD.
The LORD has punished me severely,
but he did not give me over to death.
Open to me the gates of righteousness,
that I may enter through them and give thanks to the LORD.
This is the gate of the LORD;
the righteous shall enter through it.
I thank you that you have answered me
and have become my salvation.
[All] The stone that the builders rejected has become the chief cornerstone.
This is the LORD's doing; it is marvelous in our eyes.
This is the day that the LORD has made; let us rejoice and be glad in it.
Save us, we beseech you, O LORD!
O LORD, we beseech you, give us success!
Blessed is the one who comes in the name of the LORD.
We bless you from the house of the LORD.
The LORD is God,
and he has given us light.
Bind the festal procession with branches,

up to the horns of the altar.
You are my God, and I will give thanks to you;
you are my God, I will extol you.
O give thanks to the LORD, for he is good,
for his steadfast love endures forever.
(or)
- **PSALM 150:1-6**

Praise the LORD! Praise God in his sanctuary;
praise him in his mighty firmament!
Praise him for his mighty deeds;
praise him according to his surpassing greatness!
Praise him with trumpet sound;
praise him with lute and harp!
Praise him with tambourine and dance;
praise him with strings and pipe!
Praise him with clanging cymbals;
praise him with loud clashing cymbals!
Let everything that breathes praise the LORD!
Praise the LORD!

THIRD SUNDAY OF EASTER

Acts 9:1-6 (7-20)   Psalm 30
Revelation 5:11-14   John 21:1-19

- **CALL TO WORSHIP: (Responsively)**
Sing praises to God, all of you, God's faithful ones,
We will give thanks and hallow God's name.
God's anger with our sins is but for a moment;
God's favor in Christ is for a lifetime.

- **PRAYER OF CONFESSION**
God of every tribe and language, people and nation, your dying, rising Son is the Lamb of God to take away the sins of the world. We are sinners, too, sharing with other nations and peoples, the tendency to think first of ourselves, to take whatever we can get, to give as little as possible, to be more critical of others than of ourselves, slow to forgive and to seek forgiveness. Forgive our resistance to your Holy Spirit, who is ready to help us to be obedient in deed and word, for the sake of Jesus Christ, our Savior. Amen.

- **DECLARATION OF GOD'S FORGIVENESS**
Hear the Good News! God has raised Jesus from the death of the cross and has exalted him as our leader and savior to grant us repentance and forgiveness of sins. Friends, believe the Good News! In Jesus Christ, we are forgiven.

- **EXHORTATION**
Be witnesses to all this. The Holy Spirit is given to those who are obedient to Him. Love him more than all else.

- **PRAYER OF THE DAY**
Living Christ, meet us at the place of our daily work so that what we do may be done with patience and honesty and be offered to you as our obedient service. Amen.

- **PRAYER OF THANKSGIVING**
Worthy is the Lamb that was slain to receive all power and wealth, wisdom and might, honor and glory and praise. You have purchased us at the cost of your own blood to be members of your royal house, to serve

as priests in your church, to bring your rule to this disordered earth. We rejoice in your grace that includes us in the plan to reclaim and redeem the world. We sing joyfully in anticipation of the final victory of your goodness. Amen.

• **PRAYER OF DEDICATION**
We offer to you, our prayers, our songs, our offerings that this service may be the means of caring for the flock of the Good Shepherd who laid down his life for his sheep, Jesus Christ our Lord. Amen.

• **PSALM 30**
I will extol you, O LORD, for you have drawn me up,
and did not let my foes rejoice over me.
O LORD my God, I cried to you for help,
and you have healed me.
O LORD, you brought up my soul from Sheol,
restored me to life from among those gone down to the Pit.
Sing praises to the LORD, O you his faithful ones,
and give thanks to his holy name.
For his anger is but for a moment;
his favor is for a lifetime.
Weeping may linger for the night,
but joy comes with the morning.
As for me, I said in my prosperity,
"I shall never be moved."
By your favor, O LORD, you had established me as a strong mountain;
you hid your face; I was dismayed.
To you, O LORD, I cried,
and to the LORD I made supplication:
"What profit is there in my death,
if I go down to the Pit?
Will the dust praise you?
Will it tell of your faithfulness?
Hear, O LORD, and be gracious to me!
O LORD, be my helper!"
You have turned my mourning into dancing;
you have taken off my sackcloth and clothed me with joy,
so that my soul may praise you and not be silent.
O LORD my God, I will give thanks to you forever.

FOURTH SUNDAY OF EASTER

Acts 9:36-43   Psalm 23
Revelation 7:9-17   John 10:22-30

• **CALL TO WORSHIP** (responsively)
The Lord has prepared a table before us in his house
and we are invited to dwell in the house of the LORD our whole life long.

• **PRAYER OF CONFESSION**
God our Savior, you have promised us eternal life for following the good Shepherd, your Son Jesus Christ. In the confidence that you will not let us perish, we acknowledge that we are not worthy of your care and do not follow Jesus as nearly as we should. Forgive our sins for his sake that we may rejoice with all angels and martyrs around your heavenly throne: "Salvation belongs to our God who sits upon the throne, and to the Lamb." Amen.

• **DECLARATION OF GOD'S FORGIVENESS**
Hear the Good News! Jesus gives us eternal life and promises that we will be his for ever. Friends, believe the Good News! In Jesus Christ, we are forgiven.

• **EXHORTATION**
Trust the Good Shepherd to lead you and do not look for your own way.

• **PRAYER OF THE DAY**
Give us courage, O Christ, to speak boldly in your name, whether your word is reviled or believed. Wherever we are, let your light and love shine through us so that your salvation may be brought to every locality by your Spirit within us. Amen.

• **PRAYER OF THANKSGIVING**
God beyond all time and place, God within all times and places, God eternal and universal, Blessing and glory and power and might be given to you through timeless ages. We rejoice in the hope of peace beyond times of trouble, of plenty beyond hunger and thirst, of the end of sin and grief through your cleansing and consolation. We praise the tenderness with which you wipe every tear from the eyes of those who have come

through great trouble. We are as moved by your gentleness as by your glory in Jesus Christ, your healing and humble son. Amen.

• **PRAYER OF DEDICATION**
On this first day of the week, O Christ, we make our offerings with peoples of thousands of languages and many cultural differences. You set one table in the midst of us. Draw us close to each other whenever we approach your table. Amen.

• **PSALM 23**
The LORD is my shepherd, I shall not want.
He makes me lie down in green pastures;
he leads me beside still waters;
he restores my soul.
He leads me in right paths for his name's sake.
Even though I walk through the darkest valley,
I fear no evil;
for you are with me; your rod and your staff—they comfort me.
You prepare a table before me in the presence of my enemies;
you anoint my head with oil; my cup overflows.
Surely goodness and mercy shall follow me all the days of my life,
and I shall dwell in the house of the LORD my whole life long.

FIFTH SUNDAY OF EASTER

Acts 11:1-18　　　　　　　　　　　　　　　　　Psalm 148
Revelation 21:1-6　　　　　　　　　　　　　　John 13:31-35

• **CALL TO WORSHIP: (Responsively)**
Praise the name of the Eternal One,
for God's name alone is exalted;
Praise God you who are God's people,
Young men and women alike,
old and young together!

• **PRAYER OF CONFESSION**
God of hope, you promise to make all things new, to make a new heaven and a new earth. You have been patient in your desire to restore your world to its original perfection. You have shown great forbearance to belligerent and stubborn humanity. Forgive our unwillingness to be changed, to be open to others, to open the doors of the church to those quite different from ourselves. We are sorry for the petty quarrels that spoil the resemblance the church should have to a warm and loving family. Continue your patience with us until we are mature in your love and peace, through Jesus Christ our Lord. Amen.

• **DECLARATION OF GOD'S FORGIVENESS**
Hear the Good News! We are not only baptized with water, but with the Holy Spirit. God has given us the same gift that he gave the apostles when we believed in the Lord Jesus Christ. Friends, believe the Good News! In Jesus Christ, we are forgiven.

• **EXHORTATION**
Jesus has given us a new commandment: "Love one another as I have loved you. By this all will know that you are my disciples, if you have love for one another."

• **PRAYER OF THE DAY**
Creator-God, you have come to us in this old world in Jesus of Nazareth. Teach us to love without limit and prepare us for the new heaven and earth where you will again be near enough to us to wipe away the last tear and receive us into the joyful marriage of the church with her Savior, Jesus Christ. Amen.

• PRAYER OF THANKSGIVING
When we meditate on the glorious splendor of your majesty, O God, we are inspired to proclaim the fame of your abundant goodness. You have marvellously created all things great and small. You care for the sparrow and for the spiral galaxies. Your love is more personal in Jesus Christ and none of us are forgotten. You will create again a new heaven and a new earth. Your kingdom is an everlasting kingdom and your gracious rule endures through all generations. We bless your holy name. Amen.

• PRAYER OF DEDICATION
Sovereign God, with all your works and with all your saints, we give thanks to you and bless your name. Use your church in the power of the Spirit to do more great things for the renewal of your world and all humanity through Jesus Christ. Amen.

• PSALM 148
Praise the LORD! Praise the LORD from the heavens;
praise him in the heights!
Praise him, all his angels;
praise him, all his host!
Praise him, sun and moon;
praise him, all you shining stars!
Praise him, you highest heavens,
and you waters above the heavens!
Let them praise the name of the LORD,
for he commanded and they were created.
He established them forever and ever;
he fixed their bounds, which cannot be passed.
Praise the LORD from the earth,
you sea monsters and all deeps,
fire and hail, snow and frost,
stormy wind fulfilling his command!
Mountains and all hills, fruit trees and all cedars!
Wild animals and all cattle, creeping things and flying birds!
Kings of the earth and all peoples,
princes and all rulers of the earth!
Young men and women alike,
old and young together!
Let them praise the name of the LORD,

for his name alone is exalted;
his glory is above earth and heaven.
He has raised up a horn for his people,
praise for all his faithful,
for the people of Israel who are close to him.
Praise the LORD!

SIXTH SUNDAY OF EASTER

Acts 16:9-15 Psalm 67
Revelation 21:10, 22-22:5 John 14:23-29 or 5:1-9

• CALL TO WORSHIP
Be glad and sing for joy, because God judges the peoples with justice and guides every nation on earth. May all people everywhere honor the judge unimpeachable.

• PRAYER OF CONFESSION
God of law and love, your Son came preaching that the law was made for us and not that we were made for the law. Forgive us. We have made commandments for others to follow where you have not made any. Excuse any zeal that commands what he taught rather than teaching what he commands. Recall us from any thoughtless talk and speculation, without the guidance of the Holy Spirit, that disturbs the faith and peace of mind of others. Prevent us from adding unnecessary burdens to ourselves and others when Jesus calls us to bear an easy yoke and carry a light burden, for his sake. Amen.

• DECLARATION OF GOD'S FORGIVENESS
Hear the Good News! Jesus says: Set your troubled heart at rest, and banish your fears. Peace is my gift to you. Friends, believe the Good News! In Jesus Christ, we are forgiven.

• EXHORTATION
Heed the word that God speaks through the Living Word, Jesus. Heed the word the Spirit teaches, calling to your mind the teaching of Jesus. In this way show your love for God despite those who do not heed what Jesus says.

• PRAYER OF THE DAY
Open our eyes, divine Healer, that we may see glorious visions of what you will accomplish for humanity at the end of time. Open our ears that we may hear, and open our hearts that we may heed the words that you say. Let our love for you be made evident by our readiness both to trust and to obey your guidance by the Holy Spirit. Amen.

- **PRAYER OF THANKSGIVING**
We are thankful for glimpses of blue skies through clouds of trouble, Good Creator, for visions of a beautiful city beyond the dirt and grime, the pollution and crime of our earthly cities. We long for peace amidst the tensions, the conflicts, the terrorism, the open wars of our world. We treasure the inner peace that you give us, making our survival possible in times of stress and uncertainty. We dream of the paradise of undisturbed peace, your realm of justice unshakeable, where your rule is unopposed, Monarch of peace, Prince of peace, Spirit of peace. Amen

- **PRAYER OF DEDICATION**
O God, you have blessed us with land that bears fruit after blossom time and vines that bear grapes after pruning and tying time. We offer to you our offerings in thanksgiving and our lives to be fruitful in good works that our society may not be barren and without your grace made manifest in us by the Spirit. Amen.

- **PSALM 67**
May God be gracious to us and bless us
and make his face to shine upon us,
that your way may be known upon earth,
your saving power among all nations.
Let the peoples praise you, O God;
let all the peoples praise you.
Let the nations be glad and sing for joy,
*for you judge the peoples with equity
and guide the nations upon earth.*
Let the peoples praise you, O God;
let all the peoples praise you.
The earth has yielded its increase;
God, our God, has blessed us.
May God continue to bless us;
let all the ends of the earth revere him.

ASCENSION DAY

Acts 1:1-11   Psalm 47
Ephesians 1:15-23   Luke 24:44-53

• CALL TO WORSHIP and INVOCATION
Let us worship God.
Let us pray
>that our inward eyes may be illumined
>that we may know what is the hope to which God calls us
>that we may learn how vast are the resources of the
>>Spirit's power
>
>that we may value the wealth of the heritage that we share
>>with Christ.

• SILENT PRAYER

• PRAYER OF CONFESSION
God of Moses, God of the Messiah, God of the church, forgive the doubts that plague us, the questions as to your timetable for history, the fears that the events of our time are beyond all control, even yours. Excuse our slowness in fulfilling our mission of proclaiming to all nations the name of Jesus and the repentance which brings forgiveness of sins. We need such forgiveness ourselves, for we have not properly acknowledged your majesty and power, nor received your gracious enablement to complete your work in the world. Have patience with us and the whole body of the church of which Jesus Christ is the head, in his name. Amen.

• DECLARATION OF GOD'S FORGIVENESS
Hear the Good News! Jesus sent his Father's promised gift of the Holy Spirit to arm us with power from above. Friends, believe the Good News. In Jesus Christ we are forgiven.

• EXHORTATION
Keep your minds open to understand the Scriptures, for all that was written in the Law of Moses and in the prophets and in the psalms were bound to be fulfilled in Jesus Christ. Be prepared to be a witness to all these things.

• PRAYER OF THE DAY
God of our Lord Jesus Christ, All-glorious Parent, bless us with such insightful faith that we may worship you with great joy, spending in your

house enough time to prepare us to be your witnesses everywhere in the world, by the power of the Holy Spirit. Amen.

• PRAYER OF THANKSGIVING
We praise you, Lord Christ, ascended to the right hand of Divine Sovereignty. Since your mother, Mary, bore you, you have been resplendent in holiness. The symbol for your power is the empty cross, for you have vanquished sin and death. In the Spirit you give your church powers of wisdom and vision. Thanks to you, Son of God, we are given knowledge of the Father, and thanks to you, Divine Spirit, we are given knowledge of the Son, and the inspiration to witness before the world the good news entrusted to the church. Amen.

• PRAYER OF DEDICATION
Our resources are limited, Lord God, but yours are not. What we give is multiplied beyond measure when we open ourselves to being used by the Spirit enlivening the church of the beloved Son. Amen.

• PSALM 47:1-9
Clap your hands, all you peoples;
shout to God with loud songs of joy.
For the LORD, the Most High, is awesome,
a great king over all the earth.
He subdued peoples under us,
and nations under our feet.
He chose our heritage for us,
the pride of Jacob whom he loves.
God has gone up with a shout,
the LORD with the sound of a trumpet.
Sing praises to God, sing praises;
sing praises to our King, sing praises.
For God is the king of all the earth;
sing praises with a psalm.
God is king over the nations;
God sits on his holy throne.
The princes of the peoples gather
as the people of the God of Abraham.
For the shields of the earth belong to God;
he is highly exalted.

SEVENTH SUNDAY OF EASTER

Acts 16:16-34　　　　　　　　　　　　　　　　　　Psalm 97
Revelation 22:12-14,16-17, 20-21　　　　　　　　　John 17:20-26

• **CALL TO WORSHIP: (responsively)**
Sing praises to God,
Sing praises!
For God is monarch of all the earth;
Sing praises with a psalm.

• **PRAYER OF CONFESSION**
Holy God, neither through the doors of this house nor through the gates of your eternal city may we enter worthily without your forgiveness and the washing symbolized in baptism. We need the ministry of the Spirit to create in us the desire for the finest things that life offers. Forgive our passions for lesser things unworthy of the princes and princesses of your royal house, brothers and sisters of the royal Jesus. Amen.

• **DECLARATION OF GOD'S FORGIVENESS**
Hear the Good News! Jesus prays for us who have believed in him through the word of the apostles. He prays that we may be with him where he is with the Father. Friends, believe the Good News! In Jesus Christ, we are forgiven.

• **EXHORTATION**
Keep the words of this book. Worship God who is the Alpha and Omega, the first and the last, the beginning and the end. Commit yourself to God in life and in death.

• **PRAYER OF THE DAY**
One God of one people, draw us into such close union with Jesus and with you, that all the world may know that Jesus was sent by you, to love us in your name as in his own. Fill us with overflowing love to those now feeling unloved who may learn that you have a place for them as well through Jesus our Savior. Amen.

• **PRAYER OF THANKSGIVING**
All true majesty is yours, O God. You rule over all nations. Prince of the people, you gather us around you. Eternal Spirit, you share the glory of

Jesus, the exalted Son with all who believe in him through the hearing of the gospel. *We rejoice in the privilege of calling upon your name revealed to us by Jesus Christ and the church which is his bride. We celebrate the victories you have won and have yet to win until the day of his re-appearing.* Accomplish the purposes of your love established before the creation, uniting us as one, as you are one, the Transcendent, The Incarnate, The Universal. Amen.

• PRAYER OF DEDICATION
Your gift of life is priceless, living One. We cannot repay nor match your generosity, but we can testify to your goodness through the church and personally, for the sake of Jesus Christ. Amen.

• PSALM 97
The LORD is king! Let the earth rejoice;
let the many coastlands be glad!
Clouds and thick darkness are all around him;
righteousness and justice are the foundation of his throne.
Fire goes before him, and consumes his adversaries on every side.
His lightnings light up the world; the earth sees and trembles.
The mountains melt like wax before the LORD,
before the Lord of all the earth.
The heavens proclaim his righteousness;
and all the peoples behold his glory.
All worshipers of images are put to shame,
those who make their boast in worthless idols;
all gods bow down before him.
Zion hears and is glad,
and the towns of Judah rejoice,
because of your judgments, O God.
For you, O LORD, are most high over all the earth;
you are exalted far above all gods.
The LORD loves those who hate evil;
he guards the lives of his faithful;
he rescues them from the hand of the wicked.
Light dawns for the righteous,
and joy for the upright in heart.
Rejoice in the LORD, O you righteous,
and give thanks to his holy name!

PENTECOST

Acts 2:1-21 or Genesis 11:1-9   Psalm 104:24-34, 35b
Romans 8:14-17 or Acts 2:1-21   John 14:8-17, 25-27

• CALL TO WORSHIP
Sing to the Eternal One as long as you live; praise your God while you have any breath.

• PRAYER OF CONFESSION
Universal Spirit, Human Spirit, Eternal Spirit, we confess our fear of the unknown, the strange culture, the unpredictable future, the threat of disease, of misfortune, of war, and of death. The powers of evil in the world are strong and we are anxious lest they overpower us and take us out of your hands. You have offered us the gifts of peace, the continuing instruction of the Holy Spirit but we have neglected such things as belong to our peace. Forgive us for the sake of Jesus Christ, crucified, risen, and ascended. Amen.

• DECLARATION OF GOD'S FORGIVENESS
Hear the Good News! The Holy Spirit has been sent to be our helper, to banish our fears, and to give us peace. Friends, believe the Good News! In Jesus Christ, we are forgiven.

• EXHORTATION
Have faith, the day of God's peace will come. Go forward with Christ to meet it.

• PRAYER OF THE DAY
Giver of Peace, banish our fears and our sense of loneliness. Call to our minds all that Jesus has told us and strengthen us to follow faithfully and to speak clearly of your love for all in Jesus Christ, the Savior of the World. Amen.

• PRAYER OF THANKSGIVING
Universal Mind, Universal Linguist, Universal Advocate, we are thankful that you reveal yourself in many thoughts and ideas, in many languages and varieties of music, in many ministries of teaching, worship, healing and helping. We rejoice in the work of translators that have made the Old Testament and New Testament speak our language

and more than a thousand other languages of the world. We sing your praise in many accents, in many tempos, in many harmonies, knowing that you love variety. How wonderful is the diversity in nature that you have created, God of beauty, truth, and love. Amen.

• **PRAYER OF DEDICATION**
Eternal Spirit, on this special day we give our offerings freely and gladly in the knowledge that you are at hand. You are praised today around the world, in many different places, in different languages, with multiple gifts. Receive us with our gifts, for we are yours, through Jesus Christ our Lord. Amen.

• **PSALM 104:1a, 24-34, 35b**
Bless the LORD, O my soul.
O LORD, how manifold are your works!
In wisdom you have made them all;
the earth is full of your creatures.
Yonder is the sea, great and wide,
creeping things innumerable are there,
living things both small and great.
There go the ships,
and Leviathan that you formed to sport in it.
There all look to you to give them their food in due season;
when you give to them, they gather it up;
when you open your hand, they are filled with good things.
When you hide your face, they are dismayed;
when you take away their breath, they die and return to their dust.
When you send forth your spirit, they are created;
and you renew the face of the ground.
May the glory of the LORD endure forever;
may the LORD rejoice in his works—
who looks on the earth and it trembles,
who touches the mountains and they smoke.
I will sing to the LORD as long as I live;
I will sing praise to my God while I have being.
May my meditation be pleasing to him,
for I rejoice in the LORD.
Bless the LORD, O my soul. Praise the LORD!

TRINITY SUNDAY

Proverbs 8:1-4, 22-31   Psalm 8
Romans 5:1-5   John 16:12-15

• CALL TO WORSHIP
Let us exult in the hope of the divine splendor and even in our present suffering, knowing that endurance gives proof that we have stood the test and our hope will not be mocked.

• PRAYER OF CONFESSION
God of wisdom, we have difficulty accepting ourselves as we are. We sometimes act as if we know as much as you do. At other times we put ourselves down as knowing nothing. You have given us a responsible place in the order of your creation and we sometimes abdicate that responsibility for the ecology. You have given us places of responsibility in the church, and we too often push it off on others. Forgive our irresponsibility and false pride and help us find ourselves in Jesus Christ our Lord. Amen.

• DECLARATION OF GOD'S FORGIVENESS
Hear the Good News! We have been justified through faith in Jesus Christ and have been allowed to enter the sphere of God's grace. Friends, believe the Good News! In Jesus Christ, we are forgiven.

• EXHORTATION
Let us continue at peace with God through our Lord Jesus Christ and share with others the love with which the Holy Spirit floods our hearts.

• PRAYER OF THE DAY
You have given us the Holy Spirit, Christ Jesus, to enable us to share your peace with others. Prepare us to speak your word of judgment and forgiveness as readily as we receive your judgment and forgiveness ourselves, for your own name's sake. Amen.

• PRAYER OF THANKSGIVING
Your wisdom, O God, is beyond all understanding, beyond our individual comprehension and beyond all the gathered wisdom of humanity. We are humbled by the glories of the heavens and the earth, by the powers of the wind and the tide and volcanos, by the energies of living things and

chemicals, by the complexities of the relationships of all you have created. We are grateful for all the good gifts you have given us and the grace to use them for the benefit of humanity. We are thankful for the guidance you will continue to give us as we seek new ways to recover the balance of nature and full sharing with all your creatures. We glorify you, Initiator, Investor, Integrater, one God, forever. Amen.

• PRAYER OF DEDICATION
Your greatness is seen, O Lord, our Lord, in all the world. Receive our offerings as a sign of our obedience to your mandate to manage wildlife and garden the earth, to preserve life and enrich all humanity; through Jesus Christ our Lord. Amen.

• PSALM 8:1-9
O LORD, our Sovereign, how majestic is your name in all the earth!
You have set your glory above the heavens.
Out of the mouths of babes and infants you have founded a
    bulwark because of your foes,
to silence the enemy and the avenger.
When I look at your heavens, the work of your fingers,
the moon and the stars that you have established;
what are human beings that you are mindful of them,
mortals that you care for them?
Yet you have made them a little lower than God,
and crowned them with glory and honor.
You have given them dominion over the works of your hands;
you have put all things under their feet,
all sheep and oxen, and also the beasts of the field,
the birds of the air, and the fish of the sea,
whatever passes along the paths of the seas.
O LORD, our Sovereign, how majestic is your name in all the earth!

PROPER 4

1 Kings 18:20-21, (22-29), 30-39 Psalm 96
Galatians 1:1-12 Luke 7:1-10

• **CALL TO WORSHIP**
Ascribe to the LORD, O families of the peoples, ascribe to the LORD glory and strength. Honor and majesty are before him; strength and beauty are in his sanctuary. Ascribe to the LORD the glory due his name; bring an offering, and come into his courts.

• **PRAYER OF CONFESSION**
Constant God, we confess our inconsistency. We are too often prone to seek favor with people than to risk disapproval of Christian convictions. We are prepared to rationalize or reinterpret difficult demands of Jesus and compromise our relation to him rather than put ourselves at odds with common practice. Forgive our waffling that gives an uncertain impression as to our real commitment, whether it is to the good news or popular opinion. We do trust in your mercy, through Jesus Christ the Savior. Amen.

• **DECLARATION OF GOD'S FORGIVENESS**
Hear the Good News! Our Lord Jesus Christ sacrificed himself for our sins to rescue us out of the present age of wickedness. Grace and peace are yours through Father and Son. Friends, believe the Good News! In Jesus Christ, we are forgiven.

• **EXHORTATION**
Having been called by grace, do not turn away in search of any other gospel. Don't let anyone unsettle your mind with distortions of the Good News of Christ. Be a faithful servant of Jesus.

• **PRAYER OF THE DAY**
Help us to be faithful intercessors, Good Lord, ready to pray for others as readily as for ourselves. Let our prayers reflect our humility before you. Save us from taking to ourselves any credit for the good response that you give and the great things that you do, through Jesus Christ. Amen.

- **PRAYER OF THANKSGIVING**

God of all peoples and nations, receive the praise directed to you by whatever title or name, in whatever language or ritual, by whatever race or nation. You are worthy of the highest praise, the most noble worship, the purest thought, the most precious offering of beauty and service. We thank you for the disclosure of yourself made through Jesus Christ and we are dedicated to share the good news about him with our neighbors near and far, that others may join in our hymns of thanksgiving to your name. Amen.

- **PRAYER OF DEDICATION**

Divine Savior, we cannot buy the salvation you freely give. Our offerings can help spread the good news, in word and work, in this place and every place as your people fulfill the commission given by the risen Christ. Amen.

- **PSALM 96:1-13**

O sing to the LORD a new song;
sing to the LORD, all the earth.
Sing to the LORD, bless his name;
tell of his salvation from day to day.
Declare his glory among the nations,
his marvelous works among all the peoples.
For great is the LORD, and greatly to be praised;
he is to be revered above all gods.
For all the gods of the peoples are idols,
but the LORD made the heavens.
Honor and majesty are before him;
strength and beauty are in his sanctuary.
Ascribe to the LORD, O families of the peoples,
ascribe to the LORD glory and strength.
Ascribe to the LORD the glory due his name;
bring an offering, and come into his courts.
Worship the LORD in holy splendor;
tremble before him, all the earth.
Say among the nations, "The LORD is king!
The world is firmly established;
it shall never be moved.
He will judge the peoples with equity."
Let the heavens be glad,

and let the earth rejoice;
let the sea roar, and all that fills it;
let the field exult, and everything in it.
Then shall all the trees of the forest
*sing for joy before the LORD; for he is coming,
for he is coming to judge the earth.*
He will judge the world with righteousness,
and the peoples with his truth.

PROPER 5

1 Kings 17:8-16 (17-24)　　　　　　　　　　　　Psalm 146
Galatians 1:11-24　　　　　　　　　　　　　　Luke 7:11-17

• CALL TO WORSHIP
Happy are you whose help is the God and Father of our Lord Jesus Christ and whose hope is in our God, who keeps faith forever.

• PRAYER OF CONFESSION
God of the living, we are more apt to chide you in the untimely death of a member of our families or one of our friends than to mourn what people have done to your incarnate Son Jesus of Nazareth. When you have spared our lives in serious illness, or accident, we have vowed in our thanksgiving to serve you without stint, but soon take life for granted again and forget our vows. Forgive us for the sake of him, who, for our sins, was crucified and raised from the dead, even Jesus Christ. Amen.

• DECLARATION OF GOD'S FORGIVENESS
Hear the Good News! The revelation of God's grace in Jesus Christ has been preached to both Jew and Gentile. Friends, believe the Good News. In Jesus Christ, we are forgiven.

• EXHORTATION
The Good News you have heard is not for you only, but for everyone. Pass it on.

• PRAYER OF THE DAY
Lord of life and Conqueror of death, we do not expect you to give us the power to raise the dead, but you can share your compassion with us, so that our hearts go out to the bereaved. Use us by our presence, by our words of hope, and our gestures of helpfulness, to ease their sorrow, in your name. Amen.

• PRAYER OF THANKSGIVING
Unchanging God, Man of sorrows and joy, Life-giving Spirit, we rejoice that in your favor there is life. Tears may linger until nightfall, but joy comes in the morning. When you turn your face from us we are filled with dismay, but when in Christ you smile upon us we are clothed with joy. We

strip off the sackcloth of despair and put on baptismal robes of holiness and everlasting life by the grace of our Lord Jesus Christ. Amen.

• **PRAYER OF DEDICATION**
Let us give you our life, day by day, as long as we live, timeless God, until in death you take us to higher service. Then perfect us in that service to which we are now apprenticed in Jesus Christ. Amen.

• **PSALM 146:1-10**
Praise the LORD!
Praise the LORD, O my soul!
I will praise the LORD as long as I live;
I will sing praises to my God all my life long.
Do not put your trust in princes,
in mortals, in whom there is no help.
When their breath departs, they return to the earth;
on that very day their plans perish.
Happy are those whose help is the God of Jacob,
whose hope is in the LORD their God,
who made heaven and earth,
the sea, and all that is in them;
who keeps faith forever;
who executes justice for the oppressed;
who gives food to the hungry.
The LORD sets the prisoners free;
the LORD opens the eyes of the blind.
The LORD lifts up those who are bowed down;
the LORD loves the righteous.
The LORD watches over the strangers;
he upholds the orphan and the widow,
but the way of the wicked he brings to ruin.
The LORD will reign forever,
your God, O Zion, for all generations.
Praise the LORD!

PROPER 6

1 Kings 21:1-10, (11-14), 15-21a   Psalm 5:1-8
Galatians 2:15-21   Luke 7:37-8:3

- **CALL TO WORSHIP**

Enter God's house through the abundance of God's steadfast love. Pray humbly in reverence of God's holiness. When you leave make your way straight before the eyes of God.

- **PRAYER OF CONFESSION**

Supreme Monarch, we acknowledge that we are frequently unthinking in our behavior, needing to be checked in our courses by your word in Christ, in writing, and in the witness of your church. Too often we stonewall, unwilling to confess that we could be mistaken in what we do and say. We forget the forgiveness you offer when we are honest in admitting our mistakes, our misjudgments, our misdeeds. Remind us of the increase of love that can come with the increase of forgiveness through Jesus Christ our Lord. Amen.

- **DECLARATION OF GOD'S FORGIVENESS**

Friends, hear the Good News! We are made right with God through our faith in Jesus Christ, who loved us and gave himself for us, whose death was not in vain. Friends, believe the Good News. In Jesus Christ, we are forgiven.

- **EXHORTATION**

Live by faith in the Son of God. Be crucified with Christ and let His life be lived out in you.

- **PRAYER OF THE DAY**

Merciful Lord, may all of our worship be adoration for your generous forgiveness and not an attempt to achieve what you have already granted freely. Send us out in peace of mind and heart to share your saving word in Jesus Christ our Lord. Amen.

- **PRAYER OF THANKSGIVING**

We rejoice, Good Lord, that you have cleared our account of indebtedness to God so that we may serve you in the spirit of gratitude. You have been our refuge in times of distress and have enfolded us in unfailing love. You have sent us not only critics to point out our faults but also your Son to be our Savior, not only the law but also the gospel. How great you are: holy, understanding, loving. Alleluia! Amen!

• PRAYER OF DEDICATION
Creator of beauty, Lord of life, you accept graciously not only the practical services we offer to you but also the offerings of the heart, the works of art and the gestures of love. Receive our gifts of vocation and avocation. All we have we owe to you, through Jesus Christ, our love, our Lord. Amen.

• PSALM 5:1-8
Give ear to my words, O LORD;
give heed to my sighing.
Listen to the sound of my cry, my King and my God,
for to you I pray.
O LORD, in the morning you hear my voice;
in the morning I plead my case to you, and watch.
For you are not a God who delights in wickedness;
evil will not sojourn with you.
The boastful will not stand before your eyes;
you hate all evildoers.
You destroy those who speak lies;
the LORD abhors the bloodthirsty and deceitful.
But I, through the abundance of your steadfast love, will enter your house,
I will bow down toward your holy temple in awe of you.
Lead me, O LORD, in your righteousness because of my enemies;
make your way straight before me.

PROPER 7

1 Kings 19:1-4 (5-7) 8-15a   Psalm 42 & 43
Galatians 3:23-29   Luke 8:26-39

• CALL TO WORSHIP
Come to God's dwelling as to a beacon on a holy hill. Let God's light and truth lead you. Come to the altar of God, to offer your joyful praise with heart and voice and instruments of music.

• PRAYER OF CONFESSION
Living God, you hear as well as speak, you feel as well as act. We are sometimes aware of hurting the feelings of our closest friends, but rarely do we consider that our bad behavior breaks your heart. We are too often like thoughtless children whose actions bring disgrace to the whole family. Forgive our indifference to your expectations but grant us grace to turn from our sins and to live more nearly like your Son, Jesus Christ. Amen.

• DECLARATION OF GOD'S FORGIVENESS
Hear the Good News! Through faith you are all children of God in union with Christ Jesus. Baptized into union with him, you have all put on Christ as a garment. Friends, believe the Good News! In Jesus Christ, we are forgiven.

• EXHORTATION
Leave self behind. Day after day, take up your cross and follow Christ. Only in that risk are you ultimately safe.

• PRAYER OF THE DAY
Strong Savior, give such trust in your mission that we may be less anxious for our safety and security and willing to risk more in the living out of our discipleship. We want to confirm our lip service to you in day to day obedience to your guidance, with more concern for the needs of others than the cost to ourselves. We would shoulder our own cross as you carried yours, Lord Jesus. Amen.

• PRAYER OF THANKSGIVING
God of Abraham and Sarah, God of Jesus, Mary and Joseph, God of our ancestors, we rejoice in your patience with us in the slow progress of our

social obedience as followers of Christ. In the church of your beloved Jesus Christ, we have removed the distinction between Jew and Greek, both together becoming the spiritual issue of Abraham and Sarah. After long centuries not only has the discrimination between slave and freeman being diminished, but the existence of slavery, abolished. We praise you, liberating God. We anticipate with joy the further freedom of male and female as one person in Jesus Christ. We are heirs together of the promise, redeeming God, for we belong to Christ, your only true Child, Jesus of Nazareth. Amen.

• PRAYER OF DEDICATION
Universal God, we may worship you anywhere. Let this sanctuary be not only a place of peace and sanctuary, but also a place of risk-taking and self-giving. May our offerings be an honest expression of our priorities and discipleship in the service of Jesus Christ. Amen.

• PSALMS 42 & 43
As a deer longs for flowing streams,
so my soul longs for you, O God.
My soul thirsts for God, for the living God.
When shall I come and behold the face of God?
My tears have been my food day and night,
while people say to me continually, "Where is your God?"
These things I remember, as I pour out my soul:
how I went with the throng,
and led them in procession to the house of God,
with glad shouts and songs of thanksgiving,
a multitude keeping festival.
Why are you cast down, O my soul,
and why are you disquieted within me?
Hope in God;
for I shall again praise him, my help and my God.
My soul is cast down within me;
therefore I remember you from the land of Jordan
and of Hermon, from Mount Mizar.
Deep calls to deep at the thunder of your cataracts;
all your waves and your billows have gone over me.
By day the LORD commands his steadfast love,
and at night his song is with me,
a prayer to the God of my life.

I say to God, my rock, "Why have you forgotten me?
Why must I walk about mournfully because the enemy oppresses me?"
As with a deadly wound in my body, my adversaries taunt me,
while they say to me continually, "Where is your God?"
Why are you cast down, O my soul,
and why are you disquieted within me?
Hope in God;
for I shall again praise him, my help and my God.
Vindicate me, O God,
and defend my cause against an ungodly people;
from those who are deceitful and unjust deliver me!
For you are the God in whom I take refuge;
why have you cast me off?
Why must I walk about mournfully
because of the oppression of the enemy?
O send out your light and your truth; let them lead me;
let them bring me to your holy hill and to your dwelling.
Then I will go to the altar of God, to God my exceeding joy;
and I will praise you with the harp, O God, my God.
Why are you cast down, O my soul,
and why are you disquieted within me?
Hope in God; for I shall again praise him,
my help and my God.

PROPER 8

2 Kings 2:1-2, 6-14 Psalm 77:1-2, 11-20
Galatians 5:1, 13-25 Luke 9:51-62

• **CALL TO WORSHIP (responsively)**
Call to mind the deeds of the Eternal One;
Remember the God who works wonders;
Meditate on all God's work,
And muse on the redemption of God's people.
God's way is holy.
Who is so great as our God?

• **PRAYER OF CONFESSION**
Merciful Sovereign, we are not fit subjects of your rule. You have shown us the ways of love and forgiveness but we sometimes turn back to ways of pride and hatred. We are more ready to denounce your enemies than to declare the good news. We delay obedience to your call with excuses of personal privilege. Forgive our refractory discipleship and our outright disobedience for Jesus' sake. Amen.

• **DECLARATION OF GOD'S FORGIVENESS**
Friends, hear the Good News! For freedom Christ has set us free. Through the Spirit by faith we wait for the hope of righteousness. Friends, believe the Good News! In Jesus Christ, we are forgiven.

• **EXHORTATION:**
Do not use your freedom as an opportunity for selfish advantage, but through love be servants of one another.

• **PRAYER OF THE DAY**
Deliver us, faithful Son, from deliberate delay and the excuses we use to put off positive action when you call us to follow you in service to the high purposes of God's kingdom and the completion of our Father's business. Amen.

• **PRAYER OF THANKSGIVING**
Our hearts are glad, living God, we pray with joy, for you spare our lives despite disease and accident. You are our refuge in fearful times and bring us out of shadows into the place of pleasantness and peace. We are

grateful for a goodly heritage and the noble example of the saints who have gone before us. We delight in them and in you. Amen.

• PRAYER OF DEDICATION
These gifts are meaningless, good Lord, if your name is on our lips but not in our hearts. Let your Spirit complete the good work begun in us that we may worthily bear the name of Christ. Amen.

• PSALM 77:1-2, 11-20
I cry aloud to God,
aloud to God, that he may hear me.
In the day of my trouble I seek the Lord;
in the night my hand is stretched out without wearying;
my soul refuses to be comforted.
I will call to mind the deeds of the LORD;
I will remember your wonders of old.
I will meditate on all your work,
and muse on your mighty deeds.
Your way, O God, is holy.
What god is so great as our God?
You are the God who works wonders;
you have displayed your might among the peoples.
With your strong arm you redeemed your people,
the descendants of Jacob and Joseph.
When the waters saw you, O God,
when the waters saw you, they were afraid;
the very deep trembled.
The clouds poured out water;
the skies thundered;
your arrows flashed on every side.
The crash of your thunder was in the whirlwind;
your lightnings lit up the world;
the earth trembled and shook.
Your way was through the sea,
your path, through the mighty waters;
yet your footprints were unseen.
You led your people like a flock
by the hand of Moses and Aaron.

PROPER 9

2 Kings 5:1-14   Psalm 30
Galatians 6:(1-6) 7-16   Luke 10:1-11, 16-20

- **CALL TO WORSHIP (responsively)**

Sing praises to the Eternal as God's faithful ones.
Give thanks to God's holy name,
Whose anger is but for a moment;
Whose favor is for a lifetime.

- **PRAYER OF CONFESSION**

God of justice and mercy, we complain about the harvest of our wild oats, and the sentence that is passed against our crimes. More often than not your mercy is greater than we deserve. We may not be as conspicuous as some in our misdeeds, but however subtle we are, we seek your pardon for greed and exploitation of the weak. Our dispositions are often hardhearted though you have called us to seek peace. Be open to our prayers for the sake of Jesus Christ our only Savior. Amen.

- **DECLARATION OF GOD'S FORGIVENESS**

Hear the Good News! We are granted grace, mercy and peace through our Lord Jesus Christ. Friends, believe the Good News! In Jesus Christ, we are forgiven.

- **EXHORTATION**

Wherever you go, share the word of peace, saying, "Peace be to this house." The kingdom of God has come near to you. Be sons and daughters of peace.

- **PRAYER OF THE DAY**

Send us, Lord of the harvest, into your fields of humanity to sow the seeds of peace and to seek the harvest of peace. Give us a gentle spirit even in the midst of violence and the threat of violence. In this make us like your Son, Jesus Christ. Amen.

- **PRAYER OF THANKSGIVING**

Eternal Parent, stronger than any father or mother, gentler than any father or mother, we rejoice in your care for us your children and your encircling love that seeks to draw your quarreling children into an unbroken family. We are thankful for periods of peace and places of tranquility whenever and wherever we find them. We are grateful for peacemakers, who seek to relieve tensions and propose compromises, averting violence and encouraging negotiation. We worship you, the Son of Peace, Father of peace, Mother of peace. Amen.

• PRAYER OF DEDICATION
You receive the poor and humble, merciful God, so we present our offerings mindful that all is yours and you are not restricted by what we give. May your church always be a servant people serving all in need and never devoted to power and wealth. We would serve in the same lowly way as Jesus of Nazareth. Amen.

• PSALM 30:1-12
I will extol you, O LORD, for you have drawn me up,
and did not let my foes rejoice over me.
O LORD my God, I cried to you for help,
and you have healed me.
O LORD, you brought up my soul from Sheol,
restored me to life from among those gone down to the Pit.
Sing praises to the LORD, O you his faithful ones,
and give thanks to his holy name.
For his anger is but for a moment;
his favor is for a lifetime.
Weeping may linger for the night,
but joy comes with the morning.
As for me, I said in my prosperity, "I shall never be moved."
By your favor, O LORD, you had established me as a strong mountain;
you hid your face;
I was dismayed.
To you, O LORD, I cried,
and to the LORD I made supplication:
"What profit is there in my death, if I go down to the Pit?
Will the dust praise you? Will it tell of your faithfulness?
Hear, O LORD, and be gracious to me!
O LORD, be my helper!"
You have turned my mourning into dancing;
you have taken off my sackcloth and clothed me with joy,
so that my soul may praise you and not be silent.
O LORD my God, I will give thanks to you forever.

PROPER 10

Amos 7:7-17   Psalm 82
Colossians 1:1-14   Luke 10:25-37

• CALL TO WORSHIP
Worship reverently for God is the supreme judge who is holy and absolutely just and powerful.

• PRAYER OF CONFESSION
God of law, God of grace, God of love, your plumb line condemns the bowing and tottering walls of unjust society. False religion will fail ultimately for you alone are true and to be worshipped in the Spirit of truth. Forgive any practice of ours that values other things or other persons above your worship. Pardon our infractions of your law and in your mercy grant us your Spirit to help us to live uprightly; through Jesus Christ our Lord. Amen.

• DECLARATION OF GOD'S FORGIVENESS
Hear the Good News! God has chosen to reconcile the whole world to Godself through the dear Son making peace through the shedding of his blood upon the cross. Friends, believe the Good News! In Jesus Christ, we are forgiven.

• EXHORTATION
Love the Lord your God with all your heart, with all your soul, with all your strength, and with all your mind; and your neighbor as yourself. Do that and you will live.

• PRAYER OF THE DAY
Lord of heaven and earth, on our way to your heavenly city, we want to be helpful to any who need our assistance. Save us from any false preoccupation with piety that would obscure the needs, both physical and spiritual, of our hurting neighbors. Grant us the spirit of the caring Christ. Amen.

• PRAYER OF THANKSGIVING
Invisible God in the visible Son, Creator Spirit, holding the universe together, we acclaim your preeminence. We rejoice in the resurrection of Jesus as first-born from the dead. He is the head of the church whom

we revere in worship and in daily service. We glorify you, O Creator, Sustainer, Reconciler of a fractious world. Amen.

• PRAYER OF DEDICATION
Use our gifts, gracious God, to bind up the wounded, to anoint the unnoticed with blessing, and to provide the sacraments for the church through Jesus our Savior. Amen.

• PSALM 82:1-8
God has taken his place in the divine council;
in the midst of the gods he holds judgment:
"How long will you judge unjustly
and show partiality to the wicked?
Give justice to the weak and the orphan;
maintain the right of the lowly and the destitute.
Rescue the weak and the needy;
deliver them from the hand of the wicked."
They have neither knowledge nor understanding,
they walk around in darkness;
all the foundations of the earth are shaken.
I say, "You are gods, children of the Most High, all of you;
nevertheless, you shall die like mortals,
and fall like any prince."
Rise up, O God, judge the earth;
for all the nations belong to you!

PROPER 11

Amos 8:1-12   Psalm 52
Colossians 1:15-28   Luke 10:38-42

• CALL TO WORSHIP: (responsively)
Hear the proclamation of Christ,
In whom the word of God is fully known.
Hear and be warned.
Hear and be wise.
Hear and become mature in Christ.

• PRAYER OF CONFESSION
Patient God, you still wait for us to sort out our priorities. We are often busy with trivialities avoiding confrontation of the essentials. We are bemused with the incidental and not attentive to the eternal. Forgive such preoccupation with what distracts us from your presence and does not prepare us for ultimate communion with you and yours. Amen.

• DECLARATION OF GOD'S FORGIVENESS
Hear the Good News! God has chosen to make known to you the mystery of the glory of Christ. The Spirit within you enriches your life. Friends, believe the Good News! In Jesus Christ, we are forgiven.

• EXHORTATION
Strive with all your energy to share the insights you have been given for the sake of the church in this and coming generations.

• PRAYER OF THE DAY
Capture our attention, great Teacher, that the truth you tell and the truth that you are, will be our eternal treasure never to be taken from us. Amen.

• PRAYER OF THANKSGIVING
God of surprises, we are thankful for the casual encounters in which we find you present, the shared meal and the experience of hospitality, the stories by which we come to know each other and you, the books and letters which bridge the span of centuries and the distances of our present world, the media which bring us good news as well as bad and sad. We celebrate your presence wherever and with whomever we are in the communion of the Holy Spirit and all saints through Jesus Christ. Amen.

- **PRAYER OF DEDICATION**

Let these offerings and all our gifts for strangers be made in the awareness that you are here as well as in the place of need, the hospital, the prison, the lonely room, that our giving may be more fully appropriate, given reverently and in love. Amen.

- **PSALM 52:1-9** (a psalm of judgement)

Why do you boast, O mighty one, of mischief done against the godly?
All day long you are plotting destruction.
Your tongue is like a sharp razor, you worker of treachery.
You love evil more than good, and lying more than speaking the truth.
You love all words that devour, O deceitful tongue.
But God will break you down forever;
he will snatch and tear you from your tent;
he will uproot you from the land of the living.
The righteous will see, and fear,
and will laugh at the evildoer, saying,
"See the one who would not take refuge in God,
but trusted in abundant riches, and sought refuge in wealth!"
But I am like a green olive tree in the house of God.
I trust in the steadfast love of God forever and ever.
I will thank you forever, because of what you have done.
In the presence of the faithful I will proclaim your name,
for it is good.

PROPER 12

Hosea 1:2-10   Psalm 85
Colossians 2:6-15 (16-19)   Luke 11:1-13

• CALL TO WORSHIP: (responsively)
Human as we are, let us intercede with God
for ourselves and for our sinful world,
that God will spare us from destruction
and grant us time for repentance.

• PRAYER OF CONFESSION
Listening God, Prayer-teacher, Prayer-prompter, we are often perfunctory in our prayers, casual, without expectation of response. We separate our petitions for forgiveness from the need to forgive others. We block the work of your Spirit within us, preventing the discipline that would change us and turn us outward again with persistent concern for others and ongoing intercession for the whole world, not just our own little circle. Hear our request for forgiveness. Give us a forgiving Spirit. Lord, teach us to pray. Amen

• DECLARATION OF GOD'S FORGIVENESS
Hear the Good News! God has forgiven us all our sins, cancelling the bond which pledge us to the decrees of the law, nailing it to the cross. Friends, believe the Good News. In Jesus Christ, we are forgiven.

• EXHORTATION
Live your lives in union with Jesus Christ, your Lord. Be consolidated in the faith you were taught and let your hearts overflow with thankfulness.

• PRAYER OF THE DAY
Divine Giver, you give us what is good for us. You have given us Christ and the Holy Spirit. We want to be more responsive to those gifts, with prayerful concern for others. Amen

• PRAYER OF THANKSGIVING
Infinite God, God embodied in Christ, God embodied in the church, we worship you with deep reverence. We are mystified by your invisibility and by your infinity. We believe without really understanding that your full nature could be embodied in Jesus of Nazareth, fully human, fully

divine. We wonder about the new resurrection life you offer us in our baptism that makes us alive with Christ and members of his body, the church. We are grateful for the costly victory of Christ over evil powers on the cross and rejoice in the freedom won for us. Our hearts overflow with thankfulness...

• PRAYER OF DEDICATION
Supreme Sovereign, as high as you are, you care for the lowly. Receive our humble offerings and enable us to participate with you in your unfinished work in the world; through Christ our Redeemer. Amen

• PSALM 85:1-13
LORD, you were favorable to your land;
you restored the fortunes of Jacob.
You forgave the iniquity of your people;
you pardoned all their sin.
You withdrew all your wrath;
you turned from your hot anger.
Restore us again, O God of our salvation,
and put away your indignation toward us.
Will you be angry with us forever?
Will you prolong your anger to all generations?
Will you not revive us again,
so that your people may rejoice in you?
Show us your steadfast love, O LORD,
and grant us your salvation.
Let me hear what God the LORD will speak,
for he will speak peace to his people,
to his faithful, to those who turn to him in their hearts.
Surely his salvation is at hand for those who fear him,
that his glory may dwell in our land.
Steadfast love and faithfulness will meet;
righteousness and peace will kiss each other.
Faithfulness will spring up from the ground,
and righteousness will look down from the sky.
The LORD will give what is good,
and our land will yield its increase.
Righteousness will go before him,
and will make a path for his steps.

PROPER 13

Hosea 11:1-11　　　　　　　　　　　　　　Psalm 107:1-9, 43
Colossians 3:1-11　　　　　　　　　　　　　　Luke 12:13-21

• **CALL TO WORSHIP: (responsively)**
O give thanks to the LORD, for God is good;
for God's steadfast love endures forever.
Let the redeemed of the LORD say so,
those God ransomed and gathered in from all lands.

• **PRAYER OF CONFESSION**
God above all, you may fairly judge us for living below the level of our potential. Forgive us for being only partly freed from our old natures and our sins when you have made it possible for us to be renewed in the image of yourself - the likeness in which humanity was created and which has been manifest a second time in Christ. The life we have lived is not the full resurrection-life Christ has offered us. Be patient with our slowness in putting on our new nature in Christ Jesus. Amen

• **DECLARATION OF GOD'S FORGIVENESS**
Hear the Good News! Potentially, you have died with Christ to sin, and your life is hidden with Christ in God. When Christ who is our life, is manifested, then you too will be manifested with him in glory. Friends, believe the Good News! In Jesus Christ, we are forgiven.

• **EXHORTATION**
Discard the old nature with its deeds. Put on the new nature which is constantly renewed in the image of our Maker.

• **PRAYER OF THE DAY**
Save us, merciful God, from self-destruction, from the accumulation of things for our own enjoyment only and not for the enjoyment and benefit of others. Give us the long view, the eternal perspective, that measures richness in divine and social dimensions that prepares us for the shared life of heaven in Jesus Christ. Amen.

• **PRAYER OF THANKSGIVING**
God of hope, thank you for the glimpses of glory that lift us out of despair, for the throb of life that heals the disease of the spirit, for the new virtues

that displace the old vices. We remember with gratitude the resurrection of Jesus as a sign of spiritual recovery from sin and death to eternal life. We rejoice in the new stirrings of that spiritual life in us. Praise is due to you, Living God, Living Savior, Living Spirit, for you conquer death. Amen.

• PRAYER OF DEDICATION
Creator of all life, Source of all goodness, transform these tangibles into the intangibles of the Spirit that make the church strong to do your work and accomplish your will in the Spirit of Jesus Christ. Amen.

• PSALM 107:1-9, 43
O give thanks to the LORD, for he is good;
for his steadfast love endures forever.
Let the redeemed of the LORD say so,
those he redeemed from trouble and gathered in from the lands,
from the east and from the west,
from the north and from the south.
Some wandered in desert wastes, finding no way to an inhabited town;
hungry and thirsty, their soul fainted within them.
Then they cried to the LORD in their trouble,
he led them by a straight way,
until they reached an inhabited town.
Let them thank the LORD for his steadfast love,
for his wonderful works to humankind.
For he satisfies the thirsty,
and the hungry he fills with good things.
Let those who are wise give heed to these things,
and consider the steadfast love of the LORD.

PROPER 14

Isaiah 1:1,10-20   Psalm 50:1-8, 22-23
Hebrew 11:1-3, 8-16   Luke 12:32-40

• CALL TO WORSHIP (responsively)
"Gather to me my faithful ones," invites our God,
"who have a new covenant with me by the sacrifice on the cross!"
The heavens declare the worthiness of the Lamb,
for God receives the offering of Jesus Christ.

• PRAYER OF CONFESSION
Forbearing God, despite your call for absolute obedience and the rejection of all other gods, we continue to follow old customs, unexamined behaviors, not unlike our neighbors, not in accordance with the teaching of Jesus and contrary to the law of love. Forgive such disloyal behavior that taxes your patience. Give us opportunity to mend our ways as we become aware of our need to repent and follow Jesus more nearly. We ask this in his name. Amen.

• DECLARATION OF GOD'S FORGIVENESS
Hear the Good News! It is by faith that we win God's approval. We may trust God to keep his promise. Friends, believe the Good News! In Jesus Christ, we are forgiven.

• EXHORTATION
Be ready, because the son of Man will come at an hour when you are not expecting him.

• PRAYER OF THE DAY
Keep us alert, Good Spirit, dressed for action and looking for the coming of the Son of Man. We will serve you actively in the days of your absence and with greater joy when we are fully aware of your presence with us. Amen.

• PRAYER OF THANKSGIVING
Jesus, Master, we rejoice in the appreciation you show for the simplest services we render. You have set us a perfect example of selfless service. We honor as well those like Abraham and Sarah who have followed your leading without knowing your destiny for them. We would give thanks by

our daily work as well as by our Sunday liturgy. Praise to you God of Sarah and Abraham. Praise to you, Son of Mary, Son of God. Praise to you, Spirit Eternal, without beginning, without end. Amen.

• **PRAYER OF DEDICATION**
Lord of the church, we bring our offerings Sunday by Sunday to keep the work of the church going steadily on, lest you come and find us not at our work and not prepared for your return. Amen.

• **PSALM 50:1-8, 22-23**
The mighty one, God the LORD, speaks and summons the earth
from the rising of the sun to its setting.
Out of Zion, the perfection of beauty, God shines forth.
Our God comes and does not keep silence,
before him is a devouring fire, and a mighty tempest all around him.
He calls to the heavens above and to the earth,
that he may judge his people:
"Gather to me my faithful ones,
who made a covenant with me by sacrifice!"
The heavens declare his righteousness,
for God himself is judge.
"Hear, O my people, and I will speak,
O Israel, I will testify against you.
I am God, your God. Not for your sacrifices do I rebuke you;
your burnt offerings are continually before me.
"Mark this, then, you who forget God,
or I will tear you apart, and there will be no one to deliver.
Those who bring thanksgiving as their sacrifice honor me;
to those who go the right way I will show the salvation of God."

PROPER 15

Isaiah 5:1-7   Psalm 80:1-2, 8-19
Hebrews 11:29-12:2   Luke 12:49-56

• CALL TO WORSHIP
Fix your eyes on Jesus on whom faith depends from start to finish......That will help you not to lose heart and grow faint.

• PRAYER OF CONFESSION
Steadfast God, we admit that we are easily swayed by the company we are in and their opinions. We find it difficult to speak our deeper convictions in the face of those who disagree and deride our views. We would rather be in the company of those who agree with us and need to find the courage of our convictions. Forgive our fickleness in preferring to tell people what they want to hear. Hear our prayer for the sake of your bold and truthful Son, Jesus Christ. Amen.

• DECLARATION OF GOD'S FORGIVENESS
Hear the Good News! For the sake of the joy that lay ahead of him, Jesus endured the cross, making light of its disgrace and has taken his seat at the right hand of the throne of God, where he intercedes for us. Friends, believe the Good News. In Jesus Christ, we are forgiven.

• EXHORTATION
We must throw off every encumbrance, every clinging sin, and run with resolution the race for which we are entered, our eyes fixed on Jesus, on whom faith depends from start to finish.

• PRAYER OF THE DAY
When we find ourselves separated from family and friends on issues of principle and obedience to your word, grant, God of grace, that we may be found on your side or with the humility to discover our error and to cross over to your company with Jesus Christ. Amen.

• PRAYER OF THANKSGIVING
Perfect Parent, we are grateful for the love which disciplines us, that you are not indifferent to the way we live, that you want us to learn our lessons, to improve our behavior, to share your holiness. We are thankful for the human parents, pastors, teachers, elders, friends, who have been

speaking your word to us and have been useful to you in the process of our discipline. We value the peaceful harvest of an honest life. All praise to you, spiritual Parent, exemplary Son, Holy Spirit. Amen.

• **PRAYER OF DEDICATION**
Use your church, bold Jesus, to seek justice for the weak and orphan, to see that right is done for the destitute and downtrodden, to rescue them from the power of wicked people, and to witness to all the world that you rule the nations. Amen.

• **PSALM 80:1-2, 8-19**
Give ear, O Shepherd of Israel,
you who lead Joseph like a flock!
You who are enthroned upon the cherubim,
shine forth before Ephraim and Benjamin and Manasseh.
Stir up your might, and come to save us!
You brought a vine out of Egypt;
you drove out the nations and planted it.
You cleared the ground for it;
it took deep root and filled the land.
The mountains were covered with its shade,
the mighty cedars with its branches;
it sent out its branches to the sea,
and its shoots to the River.
Why then have you broken down its walls,
so that all who pass along the way pluck its fruit?
The boar from the forest ravages it,
and all that move in the field feed on it.
Turn again, O God of hosts;
look down from heaven, and see;
have regard for this vine,
the stock that your right hand planted.
They have burned it with fire, they have cut it down;
may they perish at the rebuke of your countenance.
But let your hand be upon the one at your right hand,
the one whom you made strong for yourself.
Then we will never turn back from you;
give us life, and we will call on your name.
Restore us, O LORD God of hosts;
let your face shine, that we may be saved.

PROPER 16

Jeremiah 1:4-10   Psalm 71:1-6
Hebrews 12:18-29   Luke 13:10-17

• CALL TO WORSHIP
Come, everyone. Rejoice at all the wonderful things that Jesus has done and is doing still. Let us give thanks and offer to God an acceptable worship with reverence and awe.

• PRAYER OF CONFESSION
Holy God, there are times when we would rather not call you parent because we would prefer to live the undisciplined life. We would rather go our own way and avoid the training you insist on giving us. We like to be easy-going, slack in our morals, haphazard in our prayers, spiritually out-of-condition. Forgive such denial of our responsibilities as your children, so unlike your true and perfect Son, Jesus Christ, in whose name we pray. Amen.

• DECLARATION OF GOD'S FORGIVENESS
Hear the Good News. By the grace of our Lord Jesus Christ we are called to the assembly of the firstborn who are enrolled in heaven, and to God the judge of all, and to the spirits of the righteous made perfect, and to Jesus, the mediator of a new covenant. Friends, believe the Good News. In Jesus Christ, we are forgiven.

• EXHORTATION
Learn from Jesus that the needs of people are more important than rules.

• PRAYER OF THE DAY
Teach us your flexibility and compassion, Loving Jesus, that we may never avoid serving the needs of the sick because of some rule of propriety or anxiety about criticism from others. Amen.

• PRAYER OF THANKSGIVING
Generous and gracious God, you have given Israel a rich heritage of faith in the tradition of Abraham, Isaac, and Jacob, the footsteps of Sarah, Rebekah, and Rachel. You have given Christians an honorable name in Jesus Christ. We are glad to be included in the great gathering of the nations to your victory feast. We are happy in the promise that

there will be a new heaven and a new earth, in which we shall see your glory and worship you with people of all nations. All praise be given to you, for your love protecting us is strong and your constancy is everlasting. Praise to our Parent, stern but forgiving. Praise to your Son, older and wiser. Praise to your Spirit, who makes us brothers and sisters. Amen.

• PRAYER OF DEDICATION
As you, Holy One, received the offerings of Israel and chose some of them as priests to serve in your temple, accept our offerings as well and designate some of us to serve you in the ordained ministry so that more people and nations shall worship you. Amen.

• PSALM 71:1-6
In you, O LORD, I take refuge;
let me never be put to shame.
In your righteousness deliver me and rescue me;
incline your ear to me and save me.
Be to me a rock of refuge,
a strong fortress, to save me,
for you are my rock and my fortress.
Rescue me, O my God, from the hand of the wicked,
from the grasp of the unjust and cruel.
For you, O Lord, are my hope,
my trust, O LORD, from my youth.
Upon you I have leaned from my birth;
it was you who took me from my mother's womb.
My praise is continually of you.

PROPER 17

Jeremiah 2:4-13 Psalm 81:1, 10-16
Hebrews 13:1-8,15-16 Luke 14:1, 7-14

• **CALL TO WORSHIP**
Sing the praises of God, raise a psalm to the hallowed name... Be joyful, and exult before the Parent of the parentless, the Companion of the lonely, the One who makes a home for us all.

• **PRAYER OF CONFESSION**
Honest God, it is sometimes easier for us to be devious than straightforward. We may not tell an outright lie but may avoid disclosing the whole truth. When we are discovered as not completely trustworthy, our relationships become more cautious and uncomfortable. Forgive any pretense at being what we have not yet become. We want to have the reputation of being both fair and generous before we have fully achieved these virtues. Forgive such hypocrisy and help us to be more like your truthful and true Son, Jesus Christ. Amen.

• **DECLARATION OF GOD'S FORGIVENESS**
Hear the Good News! Jesus is mediator of the new covenant, and his sprinkled blood will purify us and make us worthy of the company of the spirits of good people made perfect. Friends, believe the Good News. In Jesus Christ, we are forgiven.

• **EXHORTATION**
As you have taken the place of humility in the confession of your sins, accept the invitation to the place of honor as one of God's children, and citizens of the heavenly city.

• **PRAYER OF THE DAY**
God above all, help us to receive such honors as come to us with modesty, and to be sincere in honoring the achievements of others in the Spirit of your Son, Jesus Christ. Amen.

• **PRAYER OF THANKSGIVING**
God of strength and compassion: we rejoice in the downfall of the wicked and the humiliation of the haughty. We exult in the raising up of the fallen and the release of the prisoner. We are thankful for the Spirit of love that

inspires your people to make a home for the friendless and provision for the poor. We are filled with gratitude as we remember the many good things you have given us to enjoy in a fruitful land and for the opportunity of sharing our plenty with others. You are patient and kind to prepare us to live together in peace in the heavenly city; through Jesus Christ our Lord. Amen.

• PRAYER OF DEDICATION
Loving God, increase in us the kindliness that is blessed in the experience of sharing. Use our gifts to start the young on the right road so that even in old age they will not leave it. Use us also to call to your way those who have not yet found it or have wandered from it; through one who is the way, the truth and the life, Jesus Christ. Amen.

• PSALM 81:1, 10-16
Sing aloud to God our strength;
shout for joy to the God of Jacob.
I am the LORD your God,
who brought you up out of the land of Egypt.
Open your mouth wide
and I will fill it.
"But my people did not listen to my voice;
Israel would not submit to me.
So I gave them over to their stubborn hearts,
to follow their own counsels.
O that my people would listen to me,
that Israel would walk in my ways!
Then I would quickly subdue their enemies,
and turn my hand against their foes.
Those who hate the LORD would cringe before him,
and their doom would last forever.
I would feed you with the finest of the wheat,
and with honey from the rock I would satisfy you."

PROPER 18

Jeremiah 18:1-11   Psalm 139:1-6, 13-18
Philemon 1-20   Luke 14:25-33

• CALL TO WORSHIP
Come and speak to our Monarch, who listens to the prayers of the lowly and will give you courage.

• PRAYER OF CONFESSION
Supreme Being from whom our being comes, only God to whom our prayers should be raised, hear our confession. We find it easier to go along with Jesus when there is a crowd. We are not always ready to part company with family and friends when our call is to costly discipleship. We may begin bravely and lose our nerve, forgetting that you can give us courage in the face of challenge and perseverance in the time of fatigue. Forgive us if we have turned back from your Son, not for the disgrace we bring on ourselves, but for the shame we bring to his name. We have no claim but his gracious intercession for us. Amen.

• DECLARATION OF GOD'S FORGIVENESS
Hear the Good News! God gives us grace and peace through Jesus Christ. Friends, believe the Good News. In Jesus Christ, we are forgiven.

• EXHORTATION
Carry your own cross and be a faithful follower of Jesus. Give up anything that prevents your being a loyal Christian.

• PRAYER OF THE DAY
Strong One, without your aid there is no way we can confront the forces of evil within us and around us. Without your enablement, there is no way we can begin, continue, and complete the work you want us to do. Discipline our spirits and keep us in the way of a disciple. Amen.

• PRAYER OF THANKSGIVING
All-knowing God, your wisdom is beyond our reach. We are thankful that you have accommodated yourself to our limited capacity in the sending of your Son into the world. We are glad for the knowledge of you that we have through Jesus of Nazareth, his life, his teaching, his healing ministry. We appreciate the patience of the Spirit who continues to teach

us as we are willing to be taught, through experience and the shared wisdom of others in talking, in reading, in listening to radio and television and recordings. We are in awe of you, for what we know, for what we can not know, for what we have yet to learn. You are the one who is, who was, and who is to come, Almighty and all wise. Amen.

• **PRAYER OF DEDICATION**
Sovereign God, you are a compassionate monarch. You hear the cries of the oppressed and have always helped the needy. You take notice of trouble and suffering and are always ready to help. Use us to do your works of mercy in the name of Jesus Christ. Amen.

• **PSALM 139:1-6, 13-18**
O LORD, you have searched me and known me.
You know when I sit down and when I rise up;
you discern my thoughts from far away.
You search out my path and my lying down,
and are acquainted with all my ways.
Even before a word is on my tongue,
O LORD, you know it completely.
You hem me in,
behind and before, and lay your hand upon me.
Such knowledge is too wonderful for me;
it is so high that I cannot attain it.
For it was you who formed my inward parts;
you knit me together in my mother's womb.
I praise you, for I am fearfully and wonderfully made.
Wonderful are your works; that I know very well.
My frame was not hidden from you,
when I was being made in secret,
intricately woven in the depths of the earth.
Your eyes beheld my unformed substance.
*In your book were written all the days that were formed for me,
when none of them as yet existed.*
How weighty to me are your thoughts, O God!
How vast is the sum of them!
I try to count them—they are more than the sand;
I come to the end—I am still with you.

PROPER 19

Jeremiah 4:11-12, 22-28   Psalm 14
1 Timothy 1:12-17   Luke 15:1-10

• CALL TO WORSHIP
Bring to the Sovereign of the ages, immortal, invisible, the only God, honor and glory. Bring to God a humble spirit, for God will not reject a humble and repentant heart.

• PRAYER OF CONFESSION
Creator God, you have every right to destroy what you have made. We have disappointed you with the decisions we have made to worship things of less value than ourselves. We have mistaken symbols for reality and have neglected the contemplation of the infinite for the finite which we can manipulate and think ourselves powerful. Whether by flood or fire, earthquake or storm, cosmic accident or man-made destruction, you could wipe us off the face of the earth. You are more patient than we deserve and relent from the threat of destruction with which you warn us in anger for our sins. Forgive us and give us time to overcome our stubbornness and intractability through Jesus Christ our Savior. Amen.

• DECLARATION OF GOD'S FORGIVENESS
Hear the Good News! We are dealt with mercifully. The grace of our Lord Jesus is lavished upon us with the faith and love which are ours through him. Friends, believe the Good News! In Jesus Christ, we are forgiven.

• EXHORTATION
Be equal to the task as you are enabled by Christ Jesus and worthy of the trust he puts in you to accomplish the service to which you are appointed.

• PRAYER OF THE DAY
Provident God, your purposes are not served by waste. You rejoice when the lost is found and the disused is put to use. Help us to share your excitement at the recovery of what was out of place and to fulfill our own ministry wherever we may serve you best; through Jesus Christ our Lord. Amen.

• PRAYER OF THANKSGIVING
We rejoice with you, happy Parent, at the return to your house of wandering children who have squandered part of their lives in meaningless living, but now are again in the circle of your adoring family. We praise your generosity in letting bygones be bygones and not casting up our past sin in our faces. Let every Eucharist be a celebration of your forgiveness and every occasion of worship a festival of your grace in Jesus Christ our Lord. Amen.

• PRAYER OF DEDICATION
Fill our minds with your wisdom, wise God, and our hearts with sincerity or our offerings are a mockery and not acceptable to you. Make us willing to obey you, to teach sinners your commands so they will turn back to you; through Jesus Christ the redeemer. Amen.

• PSALM 14:1-7
Fools say in their hearts, "There is no God."
They are corrupt, they do abominable deeds;
there is no one who does good.
The LORD looks down from heaven on humankind
to see if there are any who are wise, who seek after God.
They have all gone astray, they are all alike perverse;
there is no one who does good, no, not one.
Have they no knowledge,
*all the evildoers who eat up my people as they eat bread,
and do not call upon the LORD?*
There they shall be in great terror,
for God is with the company of the righteous.
You would confound the plans of the poor,
but the LORD is their refuge.
O that deliverance for Israel would come from Zion!
When the LORD restores the fortunes of his people,
Jacob will rejoice;
Israel will be glad.

PROPER 20

Jeremiah 8:18—9:1   Psalm 79:1-9
1 Timothy 2:1-7   Luke 16:1-13

• CALL TO WORSHIP
Praise the matchless One, servants of God. There is none like our Sovereign God in heaven or on earth...

• INVOCATION
O God of our salvation, we seek to give glory to your name through Jesus Christ and in his living Spirit. Receive our worship and hear our petitions for his sake who loved us and gave himself for us, Jesus our Lord. Amen.

• PRAYER OF CONFESSION
Ruler of All, all things, all persons, we admit that we are more shrewd in getting ahead in earthly things than we are in heavenly things. We may use every advantage we can get to avoid taxes, but not every opportunity to avoid temptation. We may pad our accounts and exaggerate our virtues in giving account of ourselves. Forgive dishonest accounting and slipshod morality for the sake of your Son, our Savior, Jesus Christ. Amen.

• PRAYER OF ASSURANCE
God our Savior, you have granted us deliverance and the forgiveness of our sins not for our worthiness but for the glory of your name. We hallow your name with thanksgiving in the Spirit who inspires our confidence. Amen.
(or)
• DECLARATION OF GOD'S FORGIVENESS
Hear the Good News! It is the will of God our Savior that all should find salvation and come to know the truth. Friends, believe the Good News. In Jesus Christ, we are forgiven.

• EXHORTATION
Be trustworthy in little things, so that God will trust you with greater things, both in this life and in the life to come.

- **PRAYER OF THE DAY**
Liberating God, free us from subjection to property, so that we may not be bound to money for the sake of power or privilege but use what we have for your purposes, the enrichment of the human spirit, others and ours; through Jesus Christ our Lord. Amen.

- **PRAYER OF THANKSGIVING**
Glorious God, People-loving Monarch, your majesty does not prevent your looking after the lowly. You sent your princely Son to live among us as our mediator. We honor the ministry of Jesus Christ and any of his disciples who have lifted the weak out of the dust and brought dignity to those who were without respect. You bring children to the childless house and make a happy family. From the rising of the sun to its setting may your name be praised, Royal One, Uncommon One, Holy One, One God. Amen.

- **PRAYER OF DEDICATION**
Timeless God, you have entered into our times in Jesus Christ and are with us now and always in the Spirit. Receive these tokens of our worldly income. We will use our money so that when it is a thing of the past, we may be received into a priceless home; through the Divine Carpenter, Jesus of Nazareth. Amen.

- **PSALM 79:1-9**
O God, the nations have come into your inheritance;
they have defiled your holy temple;
they have laid Jerusalem in ruins.
They have given the bodies of your servants to the birds of the air for food,
the flesh of your faithful to the wild animals of the earth.
They have poured out their blood like water all around Jerusalem,
and there was no one to bury them.
We have become a taunt to our neighbors,
mocked and derided by those around us.
How long, O LORD? Will you be angry forever?
Will your jealous wrath burn like fire?
Pour out your anger on the nations that do not know you,
and on the kingdoms that do not call on your name.
For they have devoured Jacob
and laid waste his habitation.

Do not remember against us the iniquities of our ancestors;
let your compassion come speedily to meet us,
for we are brought very low.
Help us, O God of our salvation, for the glory of your name;
deliver us, and forgive our sins, for your name's sake.

PROPER 21

Jeremiah 32:1-3a, 6-15   Psalm 91:1-6, 14-16
1 Timothy 6:6-19   Luke 16:19-31

• CALL TO WORSHIP
As long as you live praise the royal One, and sing praise to our God all your lives long.

• INVOCATION
All the glory of earthly monarchs pales in contrast to your majesty in both power and compassion, Immortal Sovereign. Your love in the princely Christ encourages our audience and your Spirit's inspiration enables our worship. Receive us in the name of Jesus Christ. Amen.

• PRAYER OF CONFESSION
All-seeing God, too often we close our eyes to what is going wrong in the world. We can not see with the eyes of the very poor that we live in relative luxury, even though there are others with many times what we have. We may live to eat and soothe our nerves with music. We spend more on cosmetics than some have to buy their daily bread. We escape from honest attempts at doing something to right the wrong with sentimental drama and contrived excitements. Forgive inaction so unlike the compassion and involvement of your Son, our Savior, Jesus Christ. Amen.

• PRAYER OF ASSURANCE
Gracious God, we rest secure in your initiative, coming for our salvation in Jesus Christ. May your forgiving love elicit our response of loving worship and service to you and our neighbors in the Spirit of Jesus of Nazareth. Amen.
(or)
• DECLARATION OF GOD'S FORGIVENESS
Hear the Good News! Happy is the person whose hopes are in God, who loves and restores us, straightening us out. Friends, believe the Good News. In Jesus Christ, we are forgiven.

• EXHORTATION
Run the great race of faith. Pursue justice, prayerfulness, fidelity, love, courage and gentleness. Take hold of eternal life.

• PRAYER OF THE DAY
Speaker of all languages, help us to heed the law of Moses that we may live morally, the call of the prophets that we may seek justice for all, the good news of the Risen Christ that eternal life may be the treasure that all receive through trust in your Word. Amen.

• PRAYER OF THANKSGIVING
Sovereign of sovereigns, you alone possess immortality. We are dazzled by your glory. The life you give to all living things is marvelous. To live in your presence is a great honor. To have inherited the faith of Jesus and the apostles is a priceless heritage. We would express our thankfulness by making a faithful confession in the presence of many witnesses and living faultlessly until our Lord Jesus Christ appear. Amen.

• PRAYER OF DEDICATION
Nowhere, invisible God, do we meet you more intimately than at the table of our Lord Jesus. Graciously receive our humble gifts. Transform our offerings into acts of love to one another and to the whole world; in the spirit of Jesus Christ. Amen.

• PSALM 91:1-6, 14-16
You who live in the shelter of the Most High,
who abide in the shadow of the Almighty,
will say to the LORD, "My refuge and my fortress;
my God, in whom I trust."
For he will deliver you from the snare of the fowler
and from the deadly pestilence;
he will cover you with his pinions,
and under his wings you will find refuge;
his faithfulness is a shield and buckler.
You will not fear the terror of the night,
or the arrow that flies by day,
or the pestilence that stalks in darkness,
or the destruction that wastes at noonday.
Those who love me, I will deliver;
I will protect those who know my name.
When they call to me, I will answer them;
I will be with them in trouble,
I will rescue them and honor them.
With long life I will satisfy them,
and show them my salvation.

PROPER 22

Lamentations 1:1-6 Lamentations 3:19-26 or Psalm 137
2 Timothy 1:1-14 Luke 17:5-10

• **CALL TO WORSHIP**
Let us sing of mercy and justice as we give sincere praise to God.

• **INVOCATION**
Unchanging God, your steadfast love never ceases and your mercies never come to an end. We appreciate your mercies that are new every morning; great is your faithfulness. Receive our worship as we come to you through Jesus Christ our Savior and Lord. Amen.

• **PRAYER OF CONFESSION**
Universal Judge, we are appalled at the violence and devastation that is to be seen in our world. Does our pride and opinion contribute to strife and discord that escalates into confrontation and conflict? We find it simpler to question your patience with humanity than to take some responsibility for what we could do to calm the distressed, relieve the anger of the disturbed, or pacify the hostility of the aggressive. Forgive our lack of hope that the future could be better than the past and that our faithfulness could make some difference, through your ever-hopeful Son, Jesus Christ. Amen.

• **PRAYER OF ASSURANCE**
Eternal God, we live in the light of the gospel of Jesus Christ claiming our own immortality only through the victory of the Risen One, who has broken the power of death and brought us the promise of eternal salvation. Amen.
(or)
• **DECLARATION OF GOD'S FORGIVENESS**
Hear the Good News! Our eternal salvation has been brought fully into view by the appearance on earth of our Savior, Jesus Christ, who has broken the power of death and brought immortality to light through the Gospel. Friends, believe the Good News. In Jesus Christ, we are forgiven.

• **EXHORTATION**
Stir into flame the glowing coals of the Spirit within you. The Spirit is given to you to inspire strength, love, and self-discipline.

- **PRAYER OF THE DAY**

Liberating Lord, free us from self-imposed limitations that we may go on to do what we should as your faithful servants, carrying out your orders, without expecting praise and satisfied to do our duty. Amen.

- **PRAYER OF THANKSGIVING**

Fountain of faith, your living water flows down from holy heights to replenish our thirsting spirits. We are thankful for the faith of our ancestors and for the inheritance of forms of prayer and praise that still bring meaning to our lives. We are happy in the company of others of like precious faith who lift us out of doubt and depression and despair. Fill us with such joy in believing that our faith may be drunk in by thirsting neighbors even the water of life, Jesus Christ. Amen.

- **PRAYER OF DEDICATION**

Resourceful God, our assets are not as limited as we sometimes believe. Help us to give and to use to the full all that you have given into our hands. Achieve the purposes you have had for our earth before the time of creation now fully disclosed in the advent of Christ Jesus of Nazareth. Amen.

- **LAMENTATIONS 3:19-26**

The thought of my affliction and my homelessness is wormwood
    and gall!
My soul continually thinks of it and is bowed down within me.
But this I call to mind, and therefore I have hope:
The steadfast love of the LORD never ceases,
his mercies never come to an end;
they are new every morning;
great is your faithfulness.
"The LORD is my portion," says my soul,
"therefore I will hope in him."
The LORD is good to those who wait for him, to the soul that seeks him.
It is good that one should wait quietly for the salvation of the LORD.
(or)
- **PSALM 137:1-9**

By the rivers of Babylon—there we sat down
and there we wept when we remembered Zion.
On the willows there we hung up our harps.
For there our captors asked us for songs,

and our tormentors asked for mirth,
saying, "Sing us one of the songs of Zion!"
How could we sing the LORD's song in a foreign land?
If I forget you, O Jerusalem, let my right hand wither!
Let my tongue cling to the roof of my mouth, if I do not remember you,
if I do not set Jerusalem above my highest joy.
Remember, O LORD, against the Edomites the day of Jerusalem's fall,
how they said, "Tear it down!
Tear it down! Down to its foundations!"
O daughter Babylon, you devastator!
Happy shall they be who pay you back what you have done to us!
Happy shall they be who take your little ones and dash them against the rock!

PROPER 23

Jeremiah 29:1, 4-7 Psalm 66:1-12
2 Timothy 2:8-15 Luke 17:11-19

• CALL TO WORSHIP
Bless our God, good people. May the sound of our praise be heard by our God, who has kept us among the living, and has led us on our way.

• PRAYER OF CONFESSION
Universal God, we are continually tempted to localize you, to confine you to a certain place, to a particular time, to a past experience. Forgive the limitation by our faith that does not expect you where we are, in our present and in our future as in our past; through Jesus Christ our eternal leader, who is the same yesterday, today, and forever. Amen.

• DECLARATION OF GOD'S FORGIVENESS
Hear the Good News! Even if we are faithless, Christ keeps faith, for he cannot deny himself. We too may attain the glorious and eternal salvation which is in Jesus Christ. Friends, believe the Good News! In Jesus Christ, we are forgiven.

• EXHORTATION
Try hard to show yourself worthy of God's approval, as a laborer who need not be ashamed. Be straight forward in your proclamation of the truth.

• PRAYER OF THE DAY
Compassionate Christ, as we have been touched by your love, help us to show you our thankfulness by also reaching out to others that you may touch them also through us. Amen.

• PRAYER OF THANKSGIVING
God of all places, you sent Jesus of Nazareth to show your loving presence in places of sickness, sorrow and shame, to bring healing, comfort and dignity. We are grateful for all experiences in which we encounter you. We praise your name, sender of rain and sun, maker of rainbows, light without shadow. Amen.

- **PRAYER OF DEDICATION**

Your church, connecting Spirit, is meant to be a non-profit corporation. Enable us to serve you so selflessly that the world will know that your body, the church is also willing to be broken for the sake of the world. Amen.

- **PSALM 66:1-12**

Make a joyful noise to God, all the earth;
sing the glory of his name; give to him glorious praise.
Say to God, "How awesome are your deeds!
Because of your great power, your enemies cringe before you.
All the earth worships you;
they sing praises to you, sing praises to your name."
Come and see what God has done:
he is awesome in his deeds among mortals.
He turned the sea into dry land;
they passed through the river on foot.
There we rejoiced in him,
who rules by his might forever,
whose eyes keep watch on the nations—
let the rebellious not exalt themselves.
Bless our God, O peoples,
let the sound of his praise be heard,
who has kept us among the living,
and has not let our feet slip.
For you, O God, have tested us;
you have tried us as silver is tried.
You brought us into the net;
you laid burdens on our backs;
you let people ride over our heads;
we went through fire and through water;
yet you have brought us out to a spacious place.

PROPER 24

Jeremiah 31:27-34 　　　　　　　　　　　Psalm 119:97-104
2 Timothy 3:14-4:5 　　　　　　　　　　　Luke 18:1-8

• CALL TO WORSHIP
Hear and become familiar with the sacred writings which have power to make you wise and lead you to salvation through faith in Jesus Christ.

• INVOCATION
We come to worship, O God, in response to your Word spoken in Jesus Christ and made known to us through the church of the apostles. Receive us as faithful witnesses to the Christian faith inspired by your Spirit and desiring to be found ready at the coming of the Son of humanity, Jesus Christ. Amen.

• PRAYER OF CONFESSION
Vindicator of your people, you listen to us patiently. We confess the same sins repetitiously. We trust your mercy but do not persevere in our prayer for help to overcome the faults which we confess. We have not allowed enough time for the study of scriptures as discipline in right living and as effective training for good works of every kind. Forgive our stubborn resistance to the good urging of your Spirit, for the sake of our Savior, Jesus Christ. Amen.

• PRAYER OF ASSURANCE
Merciful God, you have not forsaken us but renewed your covenant of blessing on your people, forgiving our iniquity and remembering our sins no more. We praise your name, through Jesus Christ our Savior. Amen.
(or)
• DECLARATION OF GOD'S FORGIVENESS
Hear the Good News! In the new covenant God declares: I will forgive their iniquity, and remember their sin no more. Friends, believe the Good News! In Jesus Christ, we are forgiven.

• EXHORTATION
Keep on praying and never lose heart.

- **PRAYER OF THE DAY**
Invigorating Spirit, strengthen us in the faith. Instruct our minds with the written word and enlarge our vocabulary, to speak it with conviction, to give support to all who are wavering, to challenge all who doubt. Amen.

- **PRAYER OF THANKSGIVING**
Guardian of Israel, Savior of the Church, we rejoice in your constant care. You have created a world that is magnificent, not without danger and excitement, but also with safeguards and places of rest. We are thankful for all who work for our physical health and safety. We are also glad for those who teach us your saving Word, reforming us and preparing us for judgment day. Amen.

- **PRAYER OF DEDICATION**
Like Aaron and Hur upholding the hand of Moses and the staff of God we uphold, Christ Jesus, the leaders you have called with us to lead us in your conflict with evil. Receive our gifts, our witness and our service for the victory of your monarchy. Amen.

- **PSALM 119:97-104**
Oh, how I love your law!
It is my meditation all day long.
Your commandment makes me wiser than my enemies,
for it is always with me.
I have more understanding than all my teachers,
for your decrees are my meditation.
I understand more than the aged,
for I keep your precepts.
I hold back my feet from every evil way,
in order to keep your word.
I do not turn away from your ordinances,
for you have taught me.
How sweet are your words to my taste,
sweeter than honey to my mouth!
Through your precepts I get understanding;
therefore I hate every false way.

PROPER 25

Joel 23: 23-32　　　　　　　　　　　　　　　　Psalm 65
2 Timothy 4:6-8, 16-18　　　　　　　　　　　　Luke 18:9-14

• **CALL TO WORSHIP**
Happy are you to choose to be here, having been chosen by God to be brought near to worship in God's sanctuary. Be satisfied with the goodness of this house of prayer.

• **PRAYER OF CONFESSION**
Great God, mighty and awesome, you are above all pettiness and unmoved by cheap bargaining. Forgive our stubborn narrowness. Our preference for people just like us, our suspicions about those alien to us, our double standards of caring for those of our own kind and those of our customs or races. Excuse our neglect of justice for those who need advocated because they are not in a position to speak for themselves. We have forgotten your outgoing grace, which found us when we were still strangers to you but you did not hesitate to send your only Son, Jesus to find us and include us in the number of your people. We are sorry that we are not yet much like you, over-arching God, shoulder-to-shoulder God, pervasive God. Amen.

• **DECLARATION OF GOD'S FORGIVENESS**
Hear the Good News! God has mercy on sinners, acquits them of their sins, exalting the humble. Friends, believe the Good News. In Jesus Christ, we are forgiven.

• **EXHORTATION**
Run the great race. Finish your course. Keep the faith. A garland of goodness awaits you and all who have set their hearts on Christ's appearing on that great day.

• **PRAYER OF THE DAY**
Save us from building ourselves up at the expense of others, fair God, lest we face your final put down. Teach us humility and honesty in self-evaluation that does not seek freedom from blame by doing nothing, but by striving to continue until we have completed the course you have set before us. Grant us the resurrection to final joy as you did your Son and our Savior, Jesus Christ. Amen.

• PRAYER OF THANKSGIVING
Initiating Spirit, consummating Being, you never leave your people in the lurch. You have done wonderful things which your people Israel saw with their own eyes. You are the refuge of all who come to you and their relief. You give your people strength. Your church has suffered but has never been destroyed. We rejoice in your continuing care and live in confidence that in the end the humble will be exalted and the proud be put in their place. Praise to you, the One all- knowing, the One all-feeling, the One all-healing. Amen.

• PRAYER OF DEDICATION
Whatever the offerings we place on your altar, supreme Creator, receive them as the gifts of the humble. Enable and enlarge the use of all our talents as you lead us to work together, never completely alone, for you are always with us. Amen.

• PSALM 65:1-13
Praise is due to you, O God, in Zion;
and to you shall vows be performed,
O you who answer prayer!
To you all flesh shall come.
When deeds of iniquity overwhelm us,
you forgive our transgressions.
Happy are those whom you choose
and bring near to live in your courts.
We shall be satisfied with the goodness of your house, your holy temple.
By awesome deeds you answer us with deliverance,
O God of our salvation;
you are the hope of all the ends of the earth and of the farthest seas.
By your strength you established the mountains;
you are girded with might.
You silence the roaring of the seas,
the roaring of their waves, the tumult of the peoples.
Those who live at earth's farthest bounds are awed by your signs;
you make the gateways of the morning and the evening shout for joy.
You visit the earth and water it, you greatly enrich it;
the river of God is full of water; you provide the people with grain, for so you have prepared it.
You water its furrows abundantly, settling its ridges,
softening it with showers, and blessing its growth.

You crown the year with your bounty;
your wagon tracks overflow with richness.
The pastures of the wilderness overflow,
the hills gird themselves with joy,
the meadows clothe themselves with flocks,
the valleys deck themselves with grain,
they shout and sing together for joy.

PROPER 26

Habakkuk 1:1-4; 2:1-4 Psalm 119:137-144
2 Thessalonians 1:1-4, 11-12 Luke 19:1-10

• CALL TO WORSHIP
Come in the right spirit, for the righteous live by their faith.

• PRAYER OF CONFESSION
God compassionate and gracious, longsuffering, ever constant and true, forgive our iniquity, rebellion and sin. We admit that we are only too willing to take advantage of your forgiving nature. We go on stubbornly in selfish ways and persist in sins that take their toll on generations to come. We risk our own health and the health of the unborn with the use of substances you did not create for our bodily use. We refuse your offered power to liberate us from enslaving habits. Forgive our unwillingness to change even for our health's sake; through Jesus Christ our Lord. Amen.

• DECLARATION OF GOD'S FORGIVENESS
Hear the Good News! Jesus came to pardon sinners and will bring to fulfillment every good promise and every act inspired by faith according to the grace of our God in Jesus Christ. Friends, believe the Good News. In Jesus Christ, we are forgiven.

• EXHORTATION
Live in a manner worthy of your calling so that the name of Jesus may be glorified in you, and in patient and sure expectation of his coming.

• PRAYER OF THE DAY
Universal Son of creation, in your church you have come far from Israel to seek and to save us. Send us to find those who are lost that they may find, and be found by, you and counted among the children of Abraham and Sarah, faithful believers in one God. Amen.

• PRAYER OF THANKSGIVING
Divine Searcher, you have come to where we are and we rejoice in our salvation. You are good to all and your tender care is upon all your creatures. We will talk of the glory of your peaceable kingdom and proclaim the majesty of your mighty deeds. You give with a bountiful

hand and watch over all who love you. All praise and thanksgiving we give to you, God of Abraham and Sarah, God of Jesus, Mary and Joseph, God of all the nations. Amen.

• **PRAYER OF DEDICATION**
Head of the church, we may not be rich enough to give half of what we have to charity, but we share the support of the church with other members. Grant us faith and an unselfish spirit that we may give a generous portion of what we have to others through your church and ours. Amen.

• **PSALM 119:137-144**
You are righteous, O LORD, and your judgments are right.
You have appointed your decrees in righteousness and in all faithfulness.
My zeal consumes me because my foes forget your words.
Your promise is well tried, and your servant loves it.
I am small and despised, yet I do not forget your precepts.
Your righteousness is an everlasting righteousness,
and your law is the truth.
Trouble and anguish have come upon me,
but your commandments are my delight.
Your decrees are righteous forever;
give me understanding that I may live.

PROPER 27

Haggai 1:15b—2:9 Psalm 145:1-5, 17-21 or Psalm 98
2 Thessalonians 2:13 - 3:5 Luke 20:27-38

• **CALL TO WORSHIP (responsively)**
God is near to all who pray,
to all who pray truthfully.
God fulfills the desire of all who pray devoutly;
God also hears their cry, and saves them.

• **PRAYER OF CONFESSION**
God of the living, we confess that our faith is often unimaginative. We are limited by what we know and experience in this life. We find it difficult to believe that there can be another life without the limitations of this life. We hesitate to lay up for ourselves treasures in heaven and invest too much in what passes away at the time of our death. Forgive our shortsightedness in not envisioning the glories you have prepared for your children beyond death; for the sake of your Son Jesus, who is alive from the dead. Amen.

(or)

• **PRAYER OF CONFESSION**
Faithful God, we admit that we are frequently slow to believe what you have promised through your prophets and in your Son, Jesus. We succumb to fears of death as if death were the negation of life. We live as if there is nothing to live for beyond death. We work as if there is no abiding significance to the things that we do or no loss if we choose to do nothing. Forgive our doubts, our disbelief, our unbelief, our deafness to the witness of other believers, our silence when we could give witness to the faith we have been given. Hear our prayers through our crucified but living Advocate, at your right hand, Jesus Christ our Lord. Amen.

• **DECLARATION OF GOD'S FORGIVENESS**
Hear the Good News! The Lord's love endures forever. The Lord chastens us but does not surrender us to death. God is our deliverer. Friends, believe the Good News. In Jesus Christ, we are forgiven.

• **EXHORTATION**
May the Lord direct your hearts toward God's love and the steadfastness of Christ!

- **PRAYER OF THE DAY**

God of the burning bush, Lord of the empty tomb, Spirit of life; in living prevent us from being consumed by our passions; in our dying save us from despair; and after our death raise us again to everlasting life in company with all your people. Amen.

(or)
- **PRAYER OF THE DAY**

Save us from dullness, Divine Teacher. Sharpen our wits that we may find your footsteps through all of the Scriptures, then having found them, may we follow where you lead us through this life and into the next, that we may enter the gate of the Lord as victors, living to proclaim the works of the Lord. Amen.

- **PRAYER OF THANKSGIVING**

Mighty Deliverer, you free slave nations to serve you and their neighbors in freedom. You break the bonds of death in the victory of Jesus over the grave, to free people from the fear of death, so that they may know that their lives are of eternal worth, and their work in the Spirit of abiding value. We rejoice in the Easter victory of the Savior, Jesus our Joshua, our deliverer. Amen.

(or)
- **PRAYER OF THANKSGIVING**

God of justice, compassion and love, we are grateful for all judges, legislators, and executives who are devoted to justice in action and not merely in words. We give thanks for all who have shown compassion on widows and widowers and orphans and have provided for them when they were in want. We remember happily the citizens who have welcomed newcomers strangers and aliens and helped them find their place in a new land. We celebrate in anticipation of the pleasant place you have prepared for all who love your appearing. Glory be to you, O God. Amen.

- **PRAYER OF DEDICATION**

God of the living, not only in one great hour of sharing, but in all the days of our lives, use us and our total resources to help feed the hungry, to heal the sick, to bring good news to the despondent, through Jesus Christ, our risen Lord. Amen.

(or)
- **PRAYER OF DEDICATION**

God of patriarchs and matriarchs, of kings and queens and commoners, of the married and the unmarried, though our days on earth are as a shadow, yet we seek to maintain a house to hallow your name. With honest and willing hearts we give our offerings for this abiding purpose. Amen.

• PSALM 98:1-9
O sing to the LORD a new song, for he has done marvelous things.
His right hand and his holy arm have gotten him victory.
The LORD has made known his victory;
he has revealed his vindication in the sight of the nations.
He has remembered his steadfast love and faithfulness to the house of Israel.
All the ends of the earth have seen the victory of our God.
Make a joyful noise to the LORD, all the earth;
break forth into joyous song and sing praises.
Sing praises to the LORD with the lyre,
with the lyre and the sound of melody.
With trumpets and the sound of the horn
make a joyful noise before the King, the LORD.
Let the sea roar, and all that fills it;
the world and those who live in it.
Let the floods clap their hands;
let the hills sing together for joy at the presence of the LORD,
for he is coming to judge the earth.
He will judge the world with righteousness,
and the peoples with equity.
(or)

• PSALM 145:1-5, 17-21
I will extol you, my God and King,
and bless your name forever and ever.
Every day I will bless you,
and praise your name forever and ever.
Great is the LORD, and greatly to be praised;
his greatness is unsearchable.
One generation shall laud your works to another,
and shall declare your mighty acts.
On the glorious splendor of your majesty,
and on your wondrous works, I will meditate.
The LORD is just in all his ways,
and kind in all his doings.
The LORD is near to all who call on him,

to all who call on him in truth.
He fulfills the desire of all who fear him;
he also hears their cry, and saves them.
The LORD watches over all who love him,
but all the wicked he will destroy.
My mouth will speak the praise of the LORD,
and all flesh will bless his holy name forever and ever.

PROPER 28

Isaiah 65:17-25   Isaiah 12
2 Thessalonians 3:6-13   Luke 21:5-19

• CALL TO WORSHIP
Sing praises to the Eternal One, who has done gloriously; let this be known in all the earth. Shout aloud and sing for joy, O royal priesthood, for great in your midst is the Holy One of Israel and the church.

• PRAYER OF CONFESSION
Your work, Eternal Engineer, is beyond our understanding and we do not know what it means for you to rest from your work. We confess that we are often reluctant to work. We lose the satisfaction that comes with rest after a job well done. We are too willing to let others do what we have time and opportunity to do. Forgive us, if we neglect our own work to mind other's business, if we interfere in the affairs of others instead of pulling our own weight. We forget that the night is coming when no one can work. Forgive us for the sake of your Son, the Nazarene Carpenter, who finished what you sent him to do. Amen.

• DECLARATION OF GOD'S FORGIVENESS
Hear the Good News! Surely God is your salvation; so trust, and do not be afraid. Friends, believe the Good News. In Jesus Christ, we are forgiven.

• EXHORTATION
Stand firm in the faith. Do not be misled by false prophets of doom. Do not panic when the news is bad. By standing firm you will win true life for yourselves.

• PRAYER OF THE DAY
Gentle Jesus, certain and strong, save us from uncertainty and overwhelming fears. Give us the wisdom of truth which no one can refute, and a strong voice to speak up against falsehood and slander. Though others betray us, keep us faithful to you. Amen.

• PRAYER OF THANKSGIVING
God of crisis, God of everyday, God of eternity, we prefer vistas of beauty around us but we are grateful for warning signs that make us more

attentive to the hazards of a careless road of life. *We give thanks for all who have set an example for us of certainty and assurance in the midst of trouble, conflict and disaster.* In emulating them we will come to the end of our journey rejoicing. Amen.

• PRAYER OF DEDICATION
Make us productive, Great Householder, accomplishing the work you have set before us to do. We would be about your business and provide our share of the resources needed for your church to work effectively and without pause, sustained by the eternal Spirit of Jesus Christ. Amen.

• ISAIAH 12:1-6
You will say in that day: I will give thanks to you, O LORD,
for though you were angry with me, your anger turned away,
and you comforted me.
Surely God is my salvation;
I will trust, and will not be afraid,
for the LORD GOD is my strength and my might;
he has become my salvation.
With joy you will draw water from the wells of salvation.
And you will say in that day: Give thanks to the LORD,
call on his name; make known his deeds among the nations;
proclaim that his name is exalted.
Sing praises to the LORD, for he has done gloriously;
let this be known in all the earth.
Shout aloud and sing for joy, O royal Zion,
for great in your midst is the Holy One of Israel.

CHRIST THE KING

Jeremiah 23:1-6   Luke 1:68-79
Colossians 1:11-20   Luke 23:33-43

• CALL TO WORSHIP
Follow Christ into the way of peace, for by the tender mercy of our God, the dawn from on high has broken upon us, to give light to those who sit in darkness and in the shadow of death.

• PRAYER OF CONFESSION
God of the whole universe, we confess that we often forget your concern for everyone and everything because we are so attentive to ourselves, our own families, our own congregation, our own denomination, our own country. Forgive such narrowness that ignores the magnitude of your reconciling work in Jesus Christ, King of Israel, Prince of the universe. Amen.

• DECLARATION OF GOD'S FORGIVENESS
Hear the Good News! God has chosen to reconcile the whole world by making peace through the blood shed by Jesus Christ on the cross. Friends, believe the Good News! In Jesus Christ, we are forgiven.

• EXHORTATION
Give thanks to the Parent par excellence, who has made you fit to share the heritage of God's people in the realm of life.

• PRAYER OF THE DAY
Royal One, crowned with thorns, remember us when you come into your kingdom, preparing us now by your gracious Spirit to live with you in Paradise. Amen.

• PRAYER OF THANKSGIVING
Great David's greater Son, we praise your name that you do not rule us tyrannically, but with the gentle caring of a shepherd. You have not watched over us from afar, but from the vantage point of our humanity, accepting mortality though your basic nature is unending life. Though we can not understand the wonder of your being, yet we can praise you and give thanks for the promised victory of your rule over sin and death.

King of the Jews, Prince of heaven, Sovereign of sovereigns, we worship you. Amen.

• PRAYER OF DEDICATION
Christ of God, you gave your life in making covenant with us that we should be your people and you our king. We can serve you with nothing less than our life. Amen.

• PSALM - LUKE 1:68-79
"Blessed be the Lord God of Israel,
for he has looked favorably on his people and redeemed them.
He has raised up a mighty savior for us in the house of his servant David,
as he spoke through the mouth of his holy prophets from of old,
that we would be saved from our enemies
and from the hand of all who hate us.
Thus he has shown the mercy promised to our ancestors,
and has remembered his holy covenant,
the oath that he swore to our ancestor Abraham,
to grant us that we,
being rescued from the hands of our enemies,
might serve him without fear,
in holiness and righteousness before him all our days.
And you, child, will be called the prophet of the Most High;
for you will go before the Lord to prepare his ways,
to give knowledge of salvation to his people by the
forgiveness of their sins.
By the tender mercy of our God, the dawn from on high
will break upon us,
to give light to those who sit in darkness and in the shadow of death,
to guide our feet into the way of peace."

ALL SAINTS'

Daniel 7:1-3, 15-18　　　　　　　　　　　　　　Psalm 149
Ephesians 1:11-23　　　　　　　　　　　　　　Luke 6:20-31

• **CALL TO WORSHIP**
Exult in glory, faithful people. Let the high praises of God be in your mouth, for the LORD takes pleasure in his people; and adorns the humble with victory.

• **PRAYER OF CONFESSION**
Sovereign God, we do not need nightmares to fill us with fear. The television news shows us some of the horrors of war and cruelty in the streets. When the promise of peace seems strongest new conflicts between tribes and nations breaks out and our world continues in turmoil awaiting the final victory of your justice and peace. Forgive our doubts that you will one day rule the world without opposition; through Jesus Christ our Lord. Amen.

• **DECLARATION OF GOD'S FORGIVENESS**
Hear the Good News! The Risen Christ frees you from your sins to inherit everlasting life in the glory of all the saints. Friends, believe the Good News! In Jesus Christ, we are forgiven.

• **EXHORTATION**
Pray that the God of our Lord Jesus Christ, the Father of glory, may give you a spirit of wisdom and revelation as you come to know him.

• **PRAYER OF THE DAY**
Teach us, patient Jesus, to love our enemies, and do good to those who hate us. We need the grace of your Spirit to bless those who curse us and to pray for those who abuse us. Only with your help will we do to others as we would have them do to us. Amen.

• **PRAYER OF THANKSGIVING**
Ageless God, Eternal Christ, undying Spirit, we give thanks for our inheritance in Jesus Christ with all the saints who have lived before our time and all other members of the church who live in our own time. What grace you have manifested to us sinners that we may share the glory of your unending dominion! For all who have brought that good news to

us we give you thanks. We rejoice in the communion of saints today and always. Amen.

• **PRAYER OF DEDICATION**
Eternal God, we offer ourselves as links in your communication chain to pass along the good news until the end of time. Bless your church in all that it does in obedience to your plans and purposes; through Jesus Christ our Lord. Amen.

• **PSALM 149:1-9**
Praise the LORD! Sing to the LORD a new song,
his praise in the assembly of the faithful.
Let Israel be glad in its Maker;
let the children of Zion rejoice in their King.
Let them praise his name with dancing,
making melody to him with tambourine and lyre.
For the LORD takes pleasure in his people;
he adorns the humble with victory.
Let the faithful exult in glory;
let them sing for joy on their couches.
Let the high praises of God be in their throats and
two-edged swords in their hands,
to execute vengeance on the nations and punishment on the peoples,
to bind their kings with fetters and their nobles with chains of iron,
to execute on them the judgment decreed.
This is glory for all his faithful ones.
Praise the LORD!

THANKSGIVING DAY

Deuteronomy 26:1-11   Psalm 100
Philippians 4:4-9   John 6:25-35

- **CALL TO WORSHIP**
Worship the LORD with gladness; come into his presence with singing.

- **PRAYER OF CONFESSION**
Provident God, Caring Christ, Generous Spirit, we confess that we are prone to anxiety and doubt. We forget how you have provided for us in the past and cared for our daily needs most generously. Forgive this forgetfulness and help us to take a more positive attitude of gratitude toward life in general and thankfulness for what we have rather than discontent with what we do not have, in the Spirit of the prayerful Christ our Lord. Amen.

- **DECLARATION OF GOD'S FORGIVENESS**
Hear the Good News! In Jesus Christ we have the bread of eternal life. Friends, believe the Good News! In Jesus Christ, we are forgiven.

- **EXHORTATION**
Keep on doing the things that you have learned and received and heard and seen in Christ, and the God of peace will be with you.

- **PRAYER OF THE DAY**
Caring Christ, continue to call us to the table that you spread in the world, that we may receive you anew in the breaking of the bread and the sharing of the cup and be sustained in everlasting life. Amen.

- **PRAYER OF THANKSGIVING**
Generous Creator, gracious Savior, over-flowing Spirit, you have created a magnificent planet for us to live in and an abundant harvest of land and sea. We are thankful for all that we enjoy in our own households and for the surplus that we may share with the hungry of the world. We appreciate all who are co-producers with you of the harvest and pray that we may learn even wiser ways of using and preserving the good earth you have given us with future generations in mind. Universal thanksgiving to you, O God. Amen.

- **PRAYER OF DEDICATION**

Not many of us, God of providence, produce what we can bring to you in a basket, but our financial gifts are also the fruit of our labors and we join with our neighbors in the support of this house of prayer. Receive whatever we bring through Jesus Christ your greatest gift to us. Amen.

- **PSALM 100:1-5**

Make a joyful noise to the LORD, all the earth.
Worship the LORD with gladness;
come into his presence with singing.
Know that the LORD is God.
It is he that made us, and we are his;
we are his people, and the sheep of his pasture.
Enter his gates with thanksgiving,
and his courts with praise.
Give thanks to him, bless his name.
For the LORD is good;
his steadfast love endures forever,
and his faithfulness to all generations.

INDEX FOR SCRIPTURE PASSAGES

GENESIS
11:1-9 — PENTECOST
15:1-12, 17, 18 — LENT 2
45:3-11, 15 — EPIPHANY 7

EXODUS
34:29-35 — TRANSFIGURATION

DEUTERONOMY
26:1-11 — THANKSGIVING, LENT 1

JOSHUA
5:9-12 — LENT 4

1 SAMUEL
2:18-20, 26 — CHRISTMAS + 1

1 KINGS
8:22-23, 41-43 — EPIPHANY 9
17:8-16 (17-24) — PROPER 5
18:20-21(22-29)30-39 — PROPER 4
19:1-4 (5-7) 8-15a — PROPER 7
21:1-10, (11-14), 15-21a — PROPER 6

2 KINGS
2:1-2,6-14 — PROPER 8
5:1-14 — PROPER 9

NEHEMIAH
8:1-3,5-6,8-10 — EPIPHANY 3

PSALMS
1 — EPIPHANY 6
5:1-8 — PROPER 6
8 — TRINITY
8 — NEW YEAR'S
14 — PROPER 19
19 — EPIPHANY 3
23 — EASTER 4
25:1-10 — ADVENT 1
27 — LENT 2
29 — EPIPHANY 1
30 — PROPER 9
30 — EASTER 3
31:9-16 — LENT 6 Passion
32 — LENT 4
36:5-10 — EPIPHANY 2
37:1-11, 39-40 — EPIPHANY 7
42 & 43 — PROPER 7
47 — ASCENSION
50:1-8, 22-23 — PROPER 14
51:1-17 — ASH WEDNESDAY
52 — PROPER 11
63:1-8 — LENT 3
65 — PROPER 25
66:1-12 — PROPER 23
67 — EASTER 6
71:1-6 — PROPER 16
71:1-6 — EPIPHANY 4
72:1-7,10-14 — EPIPHANY
77:1-2,11-20 — PROPER 8
79:1-9 — PROPER 20
(Alt) 80:1-7 — ADVENT 4
80:1-2, 8-19 — PROPER 15
81:1, 10-16 — PROPER 17
82 — PROPER 10
85 — PROPER 12
91:1-2, 9-16 — LENT 1
91:1-6, 14-16 — PROPER 21
92:1-4, 12-15 — EPIPHANY 8
96 — CHRISTMAS 1
96:1-9 — EPIPHANY 9
96 — PROPER 4
97 — CHRISTMAS 2
97 — EASTER 7
(Alt) 98 — PROPER 27
98 — CHRISTMAS 3
99 — TRANSFIGURATION
100 — THANKSGIVING
104:24-34, 35b — PENTECOST
107:1-9, 43 — PROPER 13
118:1-2, 14-24 — EASTER
118:1-2, 19-29 — LENT 6 (Palm)
118:14-29 — EASTER 2
119:97-104 — PROPER 24
119:137-144 — PROPER 26
126 — LENT 5
(Alt) 137 — PROPER 22
138 — EPIPHANY 5
139:1-6, 13-18 — PROPER 18
145:1-5, 17-21 — PROPER 27
146 — PROPER 5

147:12-20	CHRISTMAS +2	**LAMENTATIONS**	
148	CHRISTMAS +1	1:1-6	PROPER 22
148	EASTER 5	3:19-26	PROPER 22
149	ALL SAINTS'		
(Alt) 150	EASTER 2	**DANIEL**	
		7:1-3, 15-18	ALL SAINTS'
PROVERBS			
8:1-4, 22-31	TRINITY	**HOSEA**	
		1:2-10	PROPER 12
ECCLESIASTES		11:1-11	PROPER 13
3:1-13	NEW YEAR'S		
		JOEL	
ISAIAH		2:1-2,12-17a	ASH WEDNESDAY
1:1, 10-20	PROPER 14	2:23-32	PROPER 25
5:1-7	PROPER 15		
6:1-8 (9-13)	EPIPHANY 5	**AMOS**	
9:2-7	CHRISTMAS 1	7:7-17	PROPER 10
12	PROPER 28	8: 1-12	PROPER 11
12:2-6	ADVENT 3		
43:1-7	EPIPHANY 1	**MICAH**	
43:16-21	LENT 5	5:2-5a	ADVENT 4
50:4-9a	LENT 6 Palm,		
	LENT 6 Passion	**HABAKKUK**	
52:7-10	CHRISTMAS 3	1:1-4; 2:1-4	PROPER 26
55:1-9	LENT 3		
55:10-13	EPIPHANY 8	**ZEPHANIAH**	
(Alt) 58:1-12	ASH WEDNESDAY	3:14-20	ADVENT 3
60:1-6	EPIPHANY		
62:1-5	EPIPHANY 2	**HAGGAI**	
62:6-12	CHRISTMAS 2	1:15b-2:9	PROPER 27
65:17-25	PROPER 28		
(Alt) 65:17-25	EASTER	**MALACHI**	
		3:1-4	ADVENT 2
JEREMIAH			
1:4-10	PROPER 16,	**WISDOM OF SOLOMON**	
	EPIPHANY 4	(Alt) 10:15-21	CHRISTMAS +2
2:4-13	PROPER 17		
4:11-12, 22-28	PROPER 19	**BARUCH**	
8:18—9:1	PROPER 20	(Alt) 5:1-9	ADVENT 2
17:5-10	EPIPHANY 6		
18:1-11	PROPER 18	**SIRACH**	
23:1-6	CHRIST THE KING	(Alt) 24:1-12	CHRISTMAS +2
29:1, 4-7	PROPER 23	(Alt) 27:4-7	EPIPHANY 8
31:7-14	CHRISTMAS +2		
31:27-34	PROPER 24	**MATTHEW**	
32:1-3a, 6-15	PROPER 21	2:1-12	EPIPHANY
33:14-16	ADVENT 1	6:1-6, 16-21	ASH WEDNESDAY
		25:31-46	NEW YEAR'S

LUKE		19:28-40	LENT 6 Palm
1:47-55	ADVENT 4	20:27-38	PROPER 27
1:39-55	ADVENT 4	21:5-19	PROPER 28
1:68-79	ADVENT 2	21:25-36	ADVENT 1
1:68-79	CHRIST THE KING	22:14-23:56	LENT 6 Passion
2:1-14 (15-20)	CHRISTMAS 1	(Alt) 23:1-49	LENT 6 Passion
2:(1-7) 8-20	CHRISTMAS 2	23:33-43	CHRIST THE KING
2:41-52	CHRISTMAS +1	(Alt) 24;1-12	EASTER
3:1-6	ADVENT 2	24:44-53	ASCENSION
3:7-18	ADVENT 3		
3:15-17, 21-22	EPIPHANY 1	JOHN	
4:1-13	LENT 1	1:1-14	CHRISTMAS 3
4:14-21	EPIPHANY 3	1:(1-9) 10-18	CHRISTMAS +2
4:21-30	EPIPHANY 4	2:1-11	EPIPHANY 2
5:1-11	EPIPHANY 5	(Alt) 5:1-9	EASTER 6
6:17-26	EPIPHANY 6	6:25-35	THANKSGIVING
6:20-31	ALL SAINTS'	10:22-30	EASTER 4
6:27-38	EPIPHANY 7	12:1-8	LENT 5
6:39-49	EPIPHANY 8	13:31-35	EASTER 5
7:1-10	EPIPHANY 9	14:8-17, 25-27	PENTECOST
7:1-10	PROPER 4	14:23-29	EASTER 6
7:11-17	PROPER 5	16:12-15	TRINITY
7:37—8:3	PROPER 6	17:20-26	EASTER 7
8:26-39	PROPER 7	20:1-18	EASTER
(Alt) 9:28-36	LENT 2	20:19-31	EASTER 2
9:28-36	TRANSFIGURATION	21:1-19	EASTER 3
9:51-62	PROPER 8		
10:1-11, 16-20	PROPER 9	ACTS	
10:25-37	PROPER 10	1:1-11	ASCENSION
10:38-42	PROPER 11	2:1-21	PENTECOST
11:1-13	PROPER 12	5:27-32	EASTER 2
12:13-21	PROPER 13	8:14-17	EPIPHANY 1
12:32-40	PROPER 14	9:1-6 (7-20)	EASTER 3
12:49-56	PROPER 15	9:36-43	EASTER 4
13:1-9	LENT 3	10:34-43	EASTER
13:10-17	PROPER 16	11:1-18	EASTER 5
13:31-35	LENT 2	16:9-15	EASTER 6
14:1, 7-14	PROPER 17	16:16-34	EASTER 7
14:25-33	PROPER 18		
15:1-10	PROPER 19	ROMANS	
15:1-3, 11b-32	LENT 4	5:1-5	TRINITY
16:1-13	PROPER 20	8:14-17	PENTECOST
16:19-31	PROPER 21	10:8b-13	LENT 1
17:5-10	PROPER 22		
17:11-19	PROPER 23	1 CORINTHIANS	
18:1-8	PROPER 24	10:1-13	LENT 3
18:9-14	PROPER 25	12:1-11	EPIPHANY 2
19:1-10	PROPER 26	12:12-31a	EPIPHANY 3

13:1-13		EPIPHANY 4	**1 THESSALONIANS**	
15:1-11		EPIPHANY 5	3:9-13	ADVENT 1
15:12-20		EPIPHANY 6		
15:19-26		EASTER	**2 THESSALONIANS**	
15:35-38, 42-50		EPIPHANY 7	1:1-4, 11-12	PROPER 26
15:51-58		EPIPHANY 8	2:13—3:5	PROPER 27
			3:6-13	PROPER 28
2 CORINTHIANS				
3:12-4:2		TRANSFIGURATION	**1 TIMOTHY**	
5:16-21		LENT 4	1:12-17	PROPER 19
5:20b-6:10		ASH WEDNESDAY	2:1-7	PROPER 20
			6:6-19	PROPER 21
GALATIANS				
1:1-12		EPIPHANY 9	**2 TIMOTHY**	
1:1-12		PROPER 4	1:1-14	PROPER 22
1:11-24		PROPER 5	2:8-15	PROPER 23
2:15-21		PROPER 6	3:14-4:5	PROPER 24
3:23-29		PROPER 7	4:6-8, 16-18	PROPER 25
5:1, 13-25		PROPER 8		
6:(1-6) 7-16		PROPER 9	**TITUS**	
			2:11-14	CHRISTMAS
EPHESIANS			3:4-7	CHRISTMAS 2
1:3-14		CHRISTMAS +2		
1:11-23		ALL SAINTS'	**PHILEMON**	
1:15-23		ASCENSION	1-20	PROPER 18
3:1-12		EPIPHANY		
			HEBREWS	
PHILIPPIANS			1:1-4 (5-12)	CHRISTMAS 3
1:3-11		ADVENT 2	10:5-10	ADVENT 4
2:5-11		LENT 6 Palm,	11:1-3, 8-16	PROPER 14
		LENT 6 Passion	11:29—12:2	PROPER 15
3:4b-14		LENT 5	12:18-29	PROPER 16
3:17-4:1		LENT 2	13:1-8,15-16	PROPER 17
4:4-7		ADVENT 3		
4:4-9		THANKSGIVING	**REVELATION**	
			1:4-8	EASTER 2
COLOSSIANS			5:11-14	EASTER 3
1:1-14		PROPER 10	7:9-17	EASTER 4
1:11-20		CHRIST THE KING	21:1-6	EASTER 5
1:15-28		PROPER 11	21:1-6a	NEW YEAR'S
2:6-15 (16-19)		PROPER 12	21:10, 22-22:5	EASTER 6
3:1-11		PROPER 13	22:12-14,16-17,20-21	EASTER 7
3:12-17		CHRISTMAS +1		

Note: I am grateful to my wife Madge for her assistance in proof-reading and preparing this index. B. D. H.

A NOTE CONCERNING LECTIONARIES AND CALENDARS

The following index will aid the user of this book in matching the correct Sunday with the appropriate text during Pentecost. During the Pentecost season, this book lists Sundays by Proper (following the Revised Common and Episcopal lectionary system). Lutheran and Roman Catholic designations indicate days comparable to Sundays on which the Propers are used.

(Fixed dates do not pertain to Lutheran Lectionary)

Fixed Date Lectionaries *Common and Roman Catholic*	**Lutheran Lectionary** *Lutheran*
The Day Of Pentecost	The Day Of Pentecost
The Holy Trinity	The Holy Trinity
May 29-June 4 — Proper 4, Ordinary Time 9	Pentecost 2
June 5-11 — Proper 5, Ordinary Time 10	Pentecost 3
June 12-18 — Proper 6, Ordinary Time 11	Pentecost 4
June 19-25 — Proper 7, Ordinary Time 12	Pentecost 5
June 26-July 2— Proper 8, Ordinary Time 13	Pentecost 6
July 3-9 — Proper 9, Ordinary Time 14	Pentecost 7
July 10-16 — Proper 10, Ordinary Time 15	Pentecost 8
July 17-23 — Proper 11, Ordinary Time 16	Pentecost 9
July 24-30 — Proper 12, Ordinary Time 17	Pentecost 10
July 31-Aug. 6 — Proper 13, Ordinary Time 18	Pentecost 11
Aug. 7-13 — Proper 14, Ordinary Time 19	Pentecost 12
Aug. 14-20 — Proper 15, Ordinary Time 20	Pentecost 13
Aug. 21-27 — Proper 16, Ordinary Time 21	Pentecost 14
Aug. 28-Sept. 3 — Proper 17, Ordinary Time 22	Pentecost 15
Sept. 4-10 — Proper 18, Ordinary Time 23	Pentecost 16
Sept. 11-17 — Proper 19, Ordinary Time 24	Pentecost 17
Sept. 18-24 — Proper 20, Ordinary Time 25	Pentecost 18
Sept. 25-Oct. 1 — Proper 21, Ordinary Time 26	Pentecost 19

Oct. 2-8 — Proper 22, Ordinary Time 27	Pentecost 20
Oct. 9-15 — Proper 23, Ordinary Time 28	Pentecost 21
Oct. 16-22 — Proper 24, Ordinary Time 29	Pentecost 22
Oct. 23-29 — Proper 25, Ordinary Time 30	Pentecost 23
Oct. 30-Nov. 5 — Proper 26, Ordinary Time 31	Pentecost 24
Nov. 6-12 — Proper 27, Ordinary Time 32	Pentecost 25
Nov. 13-19 — Proper 28, Ordinary Time 33	Pentecost 26
	Pentecost 27
Nov. 20-26 — Christ The King	Christ The King

Reformation Day (or last Sunday in October) is October 31 (Common, Lutheran)

All Saints' Day (or first Sunday in November) is November 1 (Common, Lutheran, Roman Catholic)

www.ingramcontent.com/pod-product-compliance
Lightning Source LLC
Chambersburg PA
CBHW071720090426
42738CB00009B/1830